Twayne's United States Authors Series

Sylvia E. Bowman, *Editor*

INDIANA UNIVERSITY

Allen Tate

ALLEN TATE

ALLEN TATE

By FERMAN BISHOP

Illinois State University

Library of Congress Catalog Card Number: 67-21107

 **124**

Twayne Publishers, Inc. :: New York

For Katherine and William

ALLEN TATE

by

FERMAN BISHOP

Allen Tate makes the most complete examination of Tate's work yet attempted. Taking as its central idea Tate's own concept of "tension," this study scrutinizes a large number of representative writings from each phase of his career. Beginning with the *Fugitive* poems of Tate's Vanderbilt days, it shows how he quickly matured into the poet of *Mr. Pope and Other Poems*. It explores the biographies of two Southern leaders, Stonewall Jackson and Jefferson Davis. His digression into the polemics of economic and political writing as an Agrarian provides an interesting insight into a conservative intellectual's interpretation of the 1930's. Allen Tate's only novel, *The Fathers*, receives attention for its intellectual force and its use of Proustian techniques of narration. A number of his critical essays are analyzed, demonstrating the impact and range of Tate's literary contributions. But the most important part of the book is devoted to the analysis and explication of the representative poems of each phase of Tate's career, including the famous "Ode to the Confederate Dead" and "Seasons of the Soul."

Preface

ALLEN TATE is one of the most versatile man of letters in America today. He gained his earliest fame as a poet, but he is almost as well known as a critic. He has written a novel distinguished enough to rank with the best in twentieth-century American letters. He has received national attention as a political polemicist. He has written meritorious biographies of two Civil War figures. And far from the least of his activities, he has provided numerous reviews and lectures; and he has been a distinguished teacher.

This study means to provide analyses of some of the most representative works of the various periods of Tate's career. It is a work of explication because this method provides a way of keeping close to the spirit of Tate's own criticism. No doubt he will eventually be studied from many different points of view. The density of meaning in his works will easily require many studies before he is fully illuminated. But because of the difficulty of his poetry for most of his present readers, a beginning which requires that they focus attention on the works themselves seems best.

During my preparation of this volume, I have incurred more indebtedness than I can well record. But to some I wish to make especial acknowledgment. Mr. Tate himself has been unfailingly kind and generous; not only has he answered my questions, but he also opened his collection at Princeton to me. Mr. Donald Davidson and Miss Eudora Welty made a number of helpful suggestions. My colleagues have been generous with help, especially Messrs. George Canning, Victor Gimmestad, Milford Jochums, and Christopher Spencer. Mr. Jacob Steinberg of Twayne Publishers has shared some of his special knowledge of the Fugitives with me; and my long-suffering editor, Miss Sylvia Bowman, has been unfailingly helpful. I owe a great deal to the staffs of Milner Library at Illinois State University, of the library of the University of Illinois, of the library of Vanderbilt University, and of the Firestone Library of Princeton

University. My greatest debt is to my wife, who has given of her cheerfulness and encouragement at every step.

I wish to express my thanks to the following for permissions to quote from copyrighted material: quotations from *Stonewall Jackson: The Good Soldier* and *Jefferson Davis: His Rise and Fall* are used by permission of G. P. Putnam's Sons; quotations from *Collected Essays* and *The Fathers* are used by permission of Alan Swallow, Publisher; quotations from *Poems* (1960) by Allen Tate are used by permission of Charles Scribner's Sons; quotations from uncollected essays and poems in *The Fugitive* and *Jade* are used by permission of Allen Tate.

Contents

Chronology

1899   John Orley Allen Tate born, November 19, Clark County, Kentucky, son of John Orley and Eleanor Varnell Tate.

1918   Enters Vanderbilt University.

1921   Joins Donald Davidson, John Crowe Ransom and others in informal literary discussions.

1922   First issue of *The Fugitive* appears, April 12. Tate's "To Intellectual Detachment" and "Sinbad" published under the pseudonym "Henry Feathertop." Graduates from Vanderbilt University.

1923   Assumes some editorial functions of *The Fugitive*.

1924   Teaches at Lumberport, W. Va. Becomes a free-lance writer in New York. Marries Caroline Gordon, November 3 (divorced 1959).

1925   Expiration of *The Fugitive*.

1928   Contributes to *Fugitives: an Anthology of Verse*. Publishes *Mr. Pope and Other Poems* and the biography *Stonewall Jackson: The Good Soldier*.

1928-   Guggenheim Fellow. In England and France.
1929

1929   Publishes another Civil War biography, *Jefferson Davis: His Rise and Fall*.

1930   Participates in the Agrarian movement. Publishes an essay in *I'll Take my Stand; the South and the Agrarian Tradition* by Twelve Southerners.

1932   Publishes *Poems: 1928-1931*.

1932-   Southern editor, *Hound and Horn*.
1934

1933   Receives Midland Author's Prize.

1936   Publishes *The Mediterranean and Other Poems* and *Reactionary Essays on Poetry and Ideas*. Participates in another Agrarian volume: *Who Owns America? A Declaration of Independence,* edited by Allen Tate and Herbert Agar.

1937   Publishes *Selected Poems.*

1938   Publishes his only novel, *The Fathers.* Advisory Editor, *Kenyon Review.*

1938- Professor of English, Women's College of the University
1939   of North Carolina.

1939- Resident Fellow, Creative Arts Program, Princeton
1942   University.

1941   Publishes *Reason in Madness, Critical Essays.*

1943- Holds the chair of poetry in the Library of Congress.
1944

1944- Edits *The Sewanee Review.*
1946

1946- Editor of poetry and belles-lettres for Henry Holt and
1948   Company.

1948   Publishes *Poems: 1922-1947* and *On the Limits of Poetry, Selected Essays 1928-1948.*

1948- Lecturer in English, New York University.
1951

1951   Appointed Professor of English, University of Minnesota.

1953   Publishes *The Forlorn Demon: Didactic and Critical Essays.*

1956   Bollingen Prize in poetry.

1959   Publishes *Collected Essays.* Marries Isabella Gardner, August 27 (divorced Mar. 28, 1966).

1960   Publishes *Poems. The Fathers* republished in England.

1961 Receives the Brandeis University Medal for Poetry. *The Fathers* republished in the United States.

1962 Receives the Gold Medal of the Dante Society of Florence.

1963 Receives the award of the Academy of American Poets.

1964 Elected to the American Academy of Arts and Letters.

1965 Elected to the American Academy of Arts and Sciences.

1966 Marries Helen Heinz of St. Paul, Minn.

Allen Tate

Fugitive

WHEN Allen Tate was once writing about the source of one of his own poems, he admitted, "I do not know its obscure origins."[1] His observation is probably a concession to the unconscious element in poetic creation: it marks him, as he said, as a man of his age. Because this twentieth-century man is not able to claim as much for the individual as the Romantics had done, he is forced to admit a complexity of causation unknown to them. For the study of poetic origins, he must take into account the entire milieu surrounding the developing poet. Myths of precocity, inspiration, or even of genius are no longer enough to explain the development of a poet.

For the study of a writer whose mind was formed under these conditions, it is necessary to emphasize the social. And this quality of Tate's mind and art it is most essential to recognize. He has always showed an unusual sensitivity to his surroundings: he has consistently been Classical, Christian, and Southern in his outlook. If his view of the world seems less individual than that of certain other poets, it must be remembered that they, too, must have assimilated from their surroundings. Chaucer, Shakespeare, even Keats and Whitman cannot be separated from their contexts. Perhaps, then, the outlook which Allen Tate brought with him from his Kentucky background and which developed into his world-view as an artist was not very far removed from reality after all.

I *The Beginnings of* The Fugitive

During Allen Tate's undergraduate years at Vanderbilt (1918-1922) many Southern university students boiled with resentment at H. L. Mencken's "The Sahara of the Bozart." For he had written in such scathing lines as these: "If the whole of the late Confederacy were to be engulfed by a tidal wave tomorrow, the effect upon the civilized minority of men in the world would be but little greater than that of a flood on the Yang-tse-Kiang. It would be impossible in all history to match so complete a drying up of civilization."[2] The trouble was that it was so near the truth. Perhaps Mencken had not been fair to measure the cultural health of the section by its inability to bring up oboe-players, but he was certainly right in pointing out the cultural backwardness of the entire section.

No doubt the South had more pressing matters to consider than the support of symphony orchestras. The entire under-pinning of the economy was so precarious that the arts had little basis for support. The section depended upon cotton growing, which had been a depressed industry at least since 1877.[3] Few farms in the section had income enough for even a bare sufficiency. Many of the Southern people were locked in the sharecropper system; the section wasted its human resources as recklessly at it did its soil. Diseases like tuberculosis, hookworm, and pellagra were all too common. There was far too little emphasis on education. Doubtless it was rather foolish of Mencken to criticize the section for its lack of culture when it could not provide the bare necessities for its people. But the Southern college student was probably too proud to admit that. Knowing in his deepest consciousness that Mencken's harsh words spoke truly, he focused his resentment on the critic's bad manners.

Vanderbilt had heard of Mencken, and he was vehemently discussed by undergraduates like Allen Tate. He had, during his boyhood in Kentucky, had as much opportunity to observe Southern social institutions as his Tennessee classmates. As much as they, he was the product of exposure to the distinctive Southern social situation. A part of his consciousness must have been derived from his adjustment to the perils of this environment. Instead of the complacency which those in other sections could afford, Tate was forced to be aware of the existence of an ultimate chaos. Having therefore understood something of man's origin and destiny by living with their symbols, he was well prepared to acquire a poetic and philo-sophical understanding of himself and his world. Undoubtedly this fact accounts in part for his unusual ability to profit from his training at Vanderbilt.

If he understood that his world was in some sense a wasteland, he also had learned to value the oasis. Perhaps a sense of refuge was what he and his fellow Fugitives found when they banded together for their literary discussions. Certainly they were not particularly encouraged by the administration or student body at Vanderbilt. But whatever their conscious or unconscious motives for joining together, their social group was of the greatest importance for their beginnings as writers. Tate was a latecomer to the discussions, being introduced to the rest by Donald Davidson in November, 1921.

The procedures of the group were calculated to interest those seriously concerned about literature. A typical meeting might take place in the house of James Frank, a Nashville businessman devoted to the arts. John Crowe Ransom might read a poem, with carbon copies for all those present. Then would follow discussion and criticism of the poem that had been read.[4] Except for the critical abilities of the Fugitives themselves, this might have been no better than a mutual admiration society. To whom the credit should be given for keeping the level of discussion high, perhaps no one can discover. But Ransom was one of the most important, for he spoke with the authority of one who had already published. Yet he had sufficient humility to allow the give-and-take of discussion.

It is tempting to believe that Tate himself exercised a quickening influence on the group. Only four months after he began to attend the discussions, Sidney Hirsch proposed the publication of a magazine of poetry. So well had he judged the temper of the group that only a month afterward the members had accomplished the selection and editing of manuscripts, the financing, and the printing of the first *Fugitive*. The intensity of their interest becomes all the more evident when it is understood that they received almost no encouragement for their project and that they were all engaged in other occupations as well.[5]

Because *The Fugitive* proved so important as the beginning of a Southern literary renaissance, its nativity has often been regarded with solemnity. But this tone did not prevail in the first issue of the magazine. The name of the publication itself, the young men realized, might easily be misconstrued—and indeed it was later the basis of charges of escapism. Doubtless the group intended a gently ironical effect—something like that of *The Double Dealer*, the "little magazine" published in New Orleans. In accord with this tone, each of the contributors used a pseudonym—they later said not so much for concealment as for the "romance." But it seems not so much romance as gently ironic self-mockery that led John Crowe Ransom to call himself "Roger Prim"; Donald Davidson, "Robin Gallivant"; and Allen Tate, "Henry Feathertop."[6] Both the pseudonyms and the name of the magazine announced to the world a venture capable of sustaining irony.

II *Tate the Apprentice*

Tate's poems in the first *Fugitive* are so obviously apprentice work that it would be easy to dismiss them entirely. But they are worth a glance because they help to point up the beginning of his characteristic tone of expression. Of the two poems in the first issue, "Sinbad" and "To Intellectual Detachment," the latter seems the more interesting. It begins

> This is the man who classified the bits
> Of his friends' hells into a pigeonhole—
> He hung each disparate anguish on the spits
> Parboiled and roasted in his own withering soul.[7]

The far-fetched figures in this stanza and the ones that follow have much more to do with youthful high spirits than with serious poetry. Yet the reader is reminded of Thomas Mann's remark that he wrote *Buddenbrooks* out of mere playfulness.[8] For Tate too has both his playfulness and his seriousness. If he had not already heard of the idea of the dissociation of sensibility and intellect, he perceived the limitations of the scholar who cuts himself off from the possibility of thinking through his emotions. Perhaps more fundamentally, he is already in this poem trying for objectivity by "distancing." He separates the reader from the subject of the poem by the use of a *persona*. Because of the double refraction of the material of the poem, Tate's own opinions cannot be brought into focus.

This inclination to objectivity is a clear indication of the tendency away from romantic and personal self-expression that he would continue to develop in his later poetry.

The second number of *The Fugitive* contained four poems by Tate. Though he still signed himself "Henry Feathertop," he had divested himself of some of the mockery of the April number. He was obviously in search of a style, and the road he took in company with many of his fellows of the twentieth century was that of conscious imitation. Already in his poetic practice he was beginning to show the disposition of mind that would enable him to align himself with Hulme and Eliot. It was not enough for him to look into his heart and write; he must learn the poetry transmitted to him from the past and then try to find his way of making some alteration, however slight, in the whole.

The only poem of the second *Fugitive* which Tate has continued to reprint is "Farewell to Anactoria," a translation from Sappho. For some reason he did not write in sapphics, even though he had been reading Swinburne and might easily have imitated the Victorian poet's mastery of that form. Instead, he interpreted Sappho freely, using quatrains somewhat like those of Keats in "La Belle Dame Sans Merci." Unlike Keats, who used four syllables in the final verse of each stanza, Tate used six. This arrangement enabled him to retain the falling quality which Keats had achieved by the shortened final verse. But Tate's seems more restrained; there is less commitment to the emotion described than in Keats's. The lyrical qualities of the poem are illustrated well in its final lines:

> Your gleaming footstep and your grace,
> When comes another morrow,
>
> Much would I rather then behold
> Than Lydian cars or infantry.
> I beg the lot of happiness:
> Beloved in memory.[9]

The ability to amalgamate successfully the contributions of the past made it clear that young Allen Tate would be able to write the kind of poetry demanded by his generation.

III *Literary Influences: Baudelaire and Swinburne*

"In Secret Valley," which also appeared in the second *Fugitive*, bears strong resemblances to Baudelaire's prose-poem "Le Crépuscule du Soir." Both rely on a first-person narrator; both have him looking out upon a mountain scene; both exploit the twilight for its psychological possibilities; and both use certain symbols in common, such as the wind, the stars, and hell.[10] But Tate's is a far more carefully disciplined work; it has a tight dramatic structure with a definite beginning, middle, and end. And its verse pattern, too, is carefully worked out with a Swinburnian touch in alternating masculine and feminine rhymes.

The picture with which the poem begins is that of a young man standing at a window looking at a romantic scene of mountains in the distance: "Far down here the winds from off the upland blow/Sweeter and cooler, like caresses of your fingers."[11] The young man, like all romantics, makes nature suit his mood. He uses images which suggest sexual power; the winds, like Zephyrus, are associated with the energy of creativity. And the woman is present for him only as the wind is present: she ministers to his subjective need. But the picture soon becomes more complicated: "Sun has gone and furrowing; gold in the corn still lingers/I sicken of this beauty as mountains of their snow." At this time of evening twilight, the young man can look both forward and backward. The sun—associated with the reason—exists now only in his memory. The promise of spring has gone, though the beauty of the harvest is present. Werther-like, he emphasizes his decline by the comparison of himself with the mountains.

In the second stanza, he emphasizes the completeness with which the "loam" of the sunset suffuses the scene. Because it is "weary," the speaker is emphasizing the paradox that creativity is implied not so much in its promise as in its results. Yet for the human being the achievement of the created work may be a sign that creativity is gone. This paradox causes him to find the darkness in the scene a kindred quality for that in his soul.

The third stanza consists of a speech made by "ancient ghosts" —the memory. They speak in tones of self-accusation. He had formerly been a devotee of reason: day for him was "strife of brain." Long ago in the city, which is for him a Baudelaireian symbol of hell, dusk had been a time of promise. It was then associated with the woman, love, and creativity.

The fourth stanza turns to a catalog which recounts the story of a love affair. By suppressing the verbs that might have linked the nouns together, he succeeds in convincing himself, at least, of his objective view of the matter. But the affair is now over, and he employs a very homely figure to describe its end: "folded like a napkin, when the feast has come to dearth,/And hidden in the attic of dusty stars above." The connotations here make the fact of Tate's apprenticeship all too plain. Because he is not entirely sure of the condition of the young man's soul, he uses figures simply for their seeming impact. But the domestic one hardly seems to fit, and the result is even somewhat ludicrous.

The final stanza recapitulates some of the phrasing of the first; the differences between the two enable the poet to indicate the change in the speaker because of the moment of insight he has experienced. The winds, though still blowing from the same direction, are now the chilling gusts of winter. Their sounding "like the clanging of a bell" comports with the discord in his own mind. Instead of the "dusty stars" of the preceding stanza, he now sees those which are actually malevolent. Because he personifies them, it is obvious that he is using them as a reflection of himself. What he now sees is not a set of pale idealizations, but the fires of hell. Then, for the first time he notices the night birds—like Poe's raven, spirits from hell. The secret of the valley is the evil concealed beneath the exterior of its observer.

"In Secret Valley" has sufficient density for a good deal of interest, even though its themes are not highly original. Its long lines are handled much more skillfully than those of "The Raven," to which it probably owes something. Its greatest defect is its overuse of simile: Tate at this stage seems to use his figures too self-consciously. But for all its defects, this poem is a remarkable undergraduate performance.

IV *Literary Influence: Webster*

The "Horatian Epode to the Duchess of Malfi" has survived Tate's well-known penchant for revision almost exactly in the form in which it was published in the third *Fugitive* of October, 1922. This fact alone says something for the merit of the poem:

certainly a critic as discerning as Tate would hardly have allowed this poem to be reprinted so frequently if he felt it were wanting. It is especially noteworthy that this poem is built upon his assimilation of Webster. Like Eliot, Tate was reading the Jacobean dramatists.

The first line of the poem introduces a speaker who is very much aware of the element of convention in Webster's play. He says, "The stage is about to be swept of corpses."[12] There is a slight tone of mockery in his words: he is too sophisticated to be taken in by Webster's extravagant use of the Elizabethan and Jacobean tragic conventions. Yet almost in spite of himself, his words bring up the relationship of art and of life. He is aware of Shakespeare's use of metaphor and therefore of what Huizinga has called the "play element in culture."

The serious inner layer of thought in Tate's persona is suddenly exposed in the biological metaphor of the infusorian. As a modern intellectual, he is a post-Darwinian, painfully aware of the impact of science on his free will. The "you" in the second line has multiple reference. First is the Duchess; second, the speaker; and finally modern man (or even mankind) generally. This pessimism is perfectly assimilated because it expresses what scientific thought might bring to the Duchess' situation. In particular, the reference to the eohippus brings to mind Professor Marsh's famous reconstruction of the development of the horse. The primitive animal, then, symbolizes scientific views of evolution and of determinism. In the sweep of time encompassed in this interpretation of life, man, eohippus, and infusorian tend to merge in the identity of life. At the extreme of antiquity, the scavenger infusorian cannot even be certain of belonging to the animal world.

The ludicrous inconsequentiality of individual man in this scientific world disqualifies him entirely for tragedy in the Aristotelian sense. Certainly for such a creature to inflate himself with talk of "remergence with the $\overset{\prime}{o}\nu\tau\omega\varsigma$ $\overset{\prime}{o}\nu$" can only make him seem Lilliputian. Though the speaker mockingly uses the term "prattle," he has obviously raised too many important issues for easy dismissal.

In the second stanza he searches for a comparison that will enable him to understand the mystery of the Duchess' death. Though hers was not suicide, she did not take the steps that might have enabled her to stay alive. To understand her state of mind, he draws for himself a picture of a Greek girl. Her youth has encountered the skepticism of Carneades. For him there is no objective certainty; he can believe only in subjective conviction, or probability. For this girl, the shattering of the certainty of ideal love causes her to commit suicide. For the speaker, this gesture seems to typify the way in which man will react to skepticism.

In the third stanza the speaker again confronts the problem of the meaning of the Duchess' death. She, too, like the Greek girl and like the modern intellectual, has a problem of identity: she is "nameless." She, too, has to endure the waste of her promise by dying young. But instead of the histrionic gesture of the Greek girl, she dies "somewhat lovingly." And her example tells on her science-conscious modern observer. Still infected with mechanism, he interprets the dead as "skulls," without identity. But his tone now includes pity for their essential humanity. Then he indulges in some analysis of the implications of his new perspective. He finds that he still has the defect of scientific thought in the absence of an adequate teleology. But now his pessimism has become "two infinities" with the present its dividing line. To his old doubt of the future has been added a new pessimism based on the reduction of his faith in evolution.

The final brief stanza returns him to that conscious present moment in which he can rest poised between his two pessimisms. The street-cars which reassure him of that present are ironically themselves symbolic of continuity and determinism. Even though he seems secure in the boredom of this moment, it is obvious that it will not be long until his mind will again be reaching forward and back—a mind now eternally altered for its understanding of Webster's representation of the Duchess of Malfi.

V *Literary Influence: T. S. Eliot*

The importance of T. S. Eliot as an influence on Tate's undergraduate career is evident in the poem "Nuptials," published in *The Fugitive* for December, 1922. Unfortunately, the poem is not up to his best standard and has not been reprinted. But it is worth considering partly because it has some interest in itself and partly because it helps to emphasize the extent of Tate's indebtedness to Eliot. For during Tate's last year at Vanderbilt, this influence seems quite unmistakable.[13] It is, perhaps, evidence of Tate's awareness of the principle that Northrop Frye has described as the necessary continuity of poetry with itself.[14]

Even to the reader accustomed to Eliot's adaptation of the methods of Laforgue and Corbière, Tate's first lines are shocking:

> When noon-time comes the whistle blows.
> Down the straight street in jagged rows
> The multitudinous workmen shamble[15]

The harshness of the sound of the verse echoes the peremptory command of the whistle; the men are chained in a determinism of time. Then "straight street" suggests a spatial determinism as well: it recalls a similar situation in "Prufrock." And "multitudinous" emphasizes the impossibility of individuality in this situation. The second part of the stanza contains the elaboration of the unconscious reactions of the men to their imprisonment in these determinisms:

> Past Mike's saloon through swarming flies
> To the weedy lot where they may gamble
> With crooked dice and gorge stale pies.

Playing the buffoon, they use their moment of freedom to stretch their humanity out of shape; doing so compensates them for the prior distortion they have undergone in the processes of the machine. In the concluding part of the first stanza, Tate emphasizes the evil smell of the men, perhaps to show that there is some deliberateness in their offending the standards of ordinary society.

In the second stanza the poet begins to use the idea of opposites as a primary technique, as for example: "A pair of shoes balance Fate." The small versus the great, the fact versus the idea, the human being versus destiny—all these elements are built into the form as well as the thought of the verse. The unrelieved sordidness of the picture is emphasized by the use of Latinate words and surprising rhymes—both devices that were earlier used by Eliot:

> Two dollars now prognosticate
> An image supine and elate
> For Jenny sweet will keep the date
> Early or late.

The third stanza begins with the "dismal clack" of the clock—the signal to return to work. Again the men return to the grip of determinism: "They tread the same well-trodden track." But their work is not satisfying to them as human beings; for they have "a hunger flashing in the eye," which contrasts ironically with their protruding bellies. Perhaps to alleviate this spiritual hunger, one of them sings in a jazz rhythm that recalls the "Shakespeherian Rag" section of *The Waste Land.* Eliot's mockery of Goldsmith's line in the typist episode of that poem perhaps furnishes the inspiration for the parody of Henley's lines: "I am the captain of my soul/I will climb a greasy pole."

The fourth section begins with a picture of a muddy river—probably the Tennessee, but it also reminds the reader of the soiled Thames of *The Waste Land.* Repelled by the lives of the inhabitants of this land, the speaker is moved to comment in the tones of the prophetic passages of *The Waste Land:*

> I have lived many years and many lies
> But not before, on the dull stroke of seven
> Have I heard whispers on the rickety stair
> And rain upon the cracked window pane,
> Suddenly had visions of beautiful dead hair.

This passage does not ring with the compelling force of association as does Eliot's. But its connotations of illicit sexuality performed at the time of vespers and its ability to associate the sordid with the symbols of Purgatory and of baptism have a certain force. And the Laforgue-Corbière-Eliot thesis made explicit in the last line gives some justification to the idea that out of sordid ugliness can come beauty.

After a number of lines taken up with the narrator's reflections on justice and truth, there is an abrupt shift to another scene of the workman. At the sound of the whistle, he is getting up to go to work again. The marriage, if indeed it is one, has been consummated within the few hours between the cessation of the mechanical sound of his work and the present. Little wonder that he looks at Jenny and asks, "Now is she in bed dead?" Essentially, he seems to be asking whether or not he is living in a make-believe world. But to return to the world in which he must live, he puts on his overalls. And he is last seen in the hall, another of the symbols which control his life.

Death symbols are very obvious in the final stanza:

> Buzzards float upon the sky
> Shrilling a metaphysic cry,
> Machines hum, midgets play,
> Another corpse is hauled away
> Hauled away.

Probably the lines refer less to the physical death of either of the persons than to the sterility of their association. In a world of machines, man's creativity is blunted. The poem seems finally to be saying that the philosophy behind a civilization devoted merely to technical progress is death to all human values.

The major weakness of Tate's poem is that he does not achieve enough complexity of characterization to make his personages worthwhile subjects of literature. They show so little inclination to struggle that they seem rather inconsequential. He is much stronger in matters of technique: in versification, in the use of irony, and in his handling of *montage* he shows himself capable of choosing and profiting from the example of a master.

Tate was accused at this period of being merely a servile imitator of Eliot, but this was surely an overstatement of the case. For at this stage, Tate was very much the experimenter, subject to a great variety of influences as he tried the various qualities of poetic form. So intense was his interest in finding his poetic voice that he remained in Nashville working for *The Fugitive* after his graduation from Vanderbilt in 1923. No doubt he was greatly encouraged by the generous praise he had received from *The Double Dealer*. And he must have felt it all the more when he found himself commended by Eliot himself.[16]

VI *Literary Influences: Poe and Rimbaud*

The two poems published in *The Fugitive* for June-July, 1923, have both seemed to Tate worthy of reprinting. "Procession" has been more carefully reworked and has been more frequently republished, but "The Screen" is perhaps more interesting for what it shows about the poet's development at this period. The poem uses an epigraph from Poe's "The Haunted Palace," which

alerts the reader to the symbolic and subjective qualities of what
is to follow. The setting of the poem might have been taken
directly from Poe: it is a room to which only a little of the
illumination of the twilight is admitted. A single speaker is
present. Because his mind is "tired" and because this setting
does not require that he deal with ordinary reality, he allows
himself reverie about an idealized bygone time:

> Of palaces no longer golden
> Of slippered years that patter down
> Black marble stairways to the grey
> Cold silence of a broken town.[17]

The imagined splendor of this setting closely resembles that
of the monarch Thought's dominion in Poe's "The Haunted
Palace."

But the speaker begins to invest his description with a toylike
quality which tends to make his scene all the more remote and
inaccessible. The children who people his land have been defiled:

> And boys lurked once in perfumed halls,
> Cursed with ancient funerals,
> Lost in blind avenues of hair.

This passage recalls a favorite theme of Rimbaud: the boy in
search of his lost innocence. "Lurked" is associated with guilt;
"perfumed" reminds him of the seductiveness and falsity of the
woman; "halls" is both a female sex symbol and a symbol of
determinism. The curse is that which the woman always brings
—that of original sin. The boy is "lost" because he is bewildered
by the complexity of his experience and because he is now also
damned along with the woman. "Avenues of hair" is a symbol
closely akin to one from Rimbaud's "Bateau Ivre"; it suggests
the potential of the woman both for creativeness and for en-
tanglement. The implication of the entire passage is that the boy
has found both the need and the curse of creativeness in the
woman.

The mind of the speaker then returns to the present, and he
laments:

> One stricken night so endlessly
> Marted for pinnacles of stone
> Motors and steel in Tennessee.

Whereas the bygone time of his earlier reverie had been described in feminine terms, these are all masculine. Before, the speaker implies, all was full of the creative potential of the imagination. Now, he and his age along with him are dominated by the masculine. The sexual symbols of "pinnacles of stone," "motors," and "steel" set the quality of mind of the age. Its chief symbol, though, is the "cat-like limousine," which connotes an irresponsible individualism, a preoccupation with mechanism, and an effete desire for luxury.

Because such a state is so near that of death, the speaker has to reassure himself that he is not dead—that he merely suffers from the disease of aloneness of the modern. And he returns to the symbol of woman for a possible sense of renewal:

> Her eyes are open and she laughs
> Like the hard quiet in an autumn dawn,
> With lips hammered on old medallions—
> Mute souvenirs of time and war
> And beauty's vagrant cenotaphs.

This way of conceiving of the woman makes her hard; she is much less attractive than even the woman of his lost innocence. Her open eyes indicate hard rationality—the analytical faculty rather than the synthetic. Her laughter is too controlled for emotion: the synaesthesia of "hard quiet" reveals her total commitment to intellectuality. To reinforce the speaker's interpretation of the masculine and military elements in her personality, Tate added in the revision published in *Mr. Pope and Other Poems* the line: "Her mouth is a cold and faultless scar."

The next section of the poem develops the speaker's reaction to the portrait of the woman just completed. If she is merely the product of his imagining, then perhaps he can do something to make creativity possible once more:

> I will seek the golden blood
> Of rivers, at sunset; I will drink.
> For a thirst of golden hair,
> I will drink with the evening star.

But he cannot forget that he is a modern man who must "walk a fearful road." For him a vision must pass "like the headlong flash of a motor car." The very form of his thought is controlled by his age. His awareness of his difficulty leads him to ask whether or not "night" will be filled with the forms of his imagination: essentially, he is asking Hamlet's question once again. And when he forces himself to face up to the possibility of the death of the woman, he realizes that for all her hardness and cruelty "spring will not burst" for him when this occurs. Reality for him must be colored by the condition of his own mind, and because of his subjective condition

> the night
> Falls down from bitter stars and palls
> The mind descanting to the dark
> Of boys and girls and golden rivers.

In the final section of resolution, a hand symbolism predominates:

> Hope I have clutched beyond death,
> Stretched fingers down a street for light,
> Panted for a stronger breath—
> Cast jewels into a desolate sea.

In his search for illumination, he is using consciously controlled acts of will. But after each attempt come dusk and the after-dinner hour. Then the formula of his memory pattern is repeated, and the emotional takes precedence over the rational. The climax of these emotional moments of the evening comes with "the ivory hand/I have lived for, a lonely customer." This is the woman's hand, symbolic of her humanity and femininity, yet for him neither quite human nor feminine. He knows enough to disparage his crude system of values, but he concludes pessimistically because it is not possible for his reason to maintain entire control over his emotions.

VII   *The Accomplishment of the Fugitive Period*

The density of meaning which shows up so clearly in close analysis of some of the poems of Tate's Fugitive period emphasizes the remarkable quality of his accomplishment while at Vanderbilt. Within two or three years, he acquired the formidable intellectual materials and the tightly disciplined style of his school of poetry. When he came to Vanderbilt, he doubtless had considerable learning and experience; but he had not used his accomplishment in a way that would indicate its promise. In his earliest published work, "A Ballade of the Lugubrious Wench," he obviously did not intend to write serious poetry, but it is worth examining as an indication of Tate's early promise. Its second stanza contains these lines:

> Gone from home the sailor is going
> Over the green wave, flouting skies,
> Till in Bombay two wives meet—knowing!
> And scorch his laughter to ashy sighs![18]

There is not much in these lines to distinguish them from the ordinary undergraduate performance: the high spirits are there, but so are the faltering rhythms.

How much more control he had acquired by 1924 might be illustrated by the following lines from "Touselled," which appeared in the third volume of *The Fugitive:*

> Unhappily fractured music in the scene
> Spills a hollow bird, perched
> On the bony Fall. Drip drip
> Sharply, vertically sharp the drops
> Plunged from the eaves. No wonder an interval
>
> Stalked by twin demons, Day and Night,
> Is defeated.[19]

Though it is manifestly unfair to load the scales by comparing poems written for very different purposes, the consistency of rhythm and the tightness of control of the second poem were probably not available to the writer of the first. Clearly, Tate had taken seriously his apprenticeship to poetry at Vanderbilt and had acquired a remarkable maturity of style within a very brief period.

Perhaps it is futile to inquire into the reasons for this development: creativity is a quality too rare to be easily understood. Tate himself has sometimes fallen back on the term "genius" when writing of his fellow-Fugitives. But this explanation always seems too easy, and it seems particularly difficult to use of a group. It seems highly improbable that so considerable a number of poetic geniuses should have accidentally come together on a campus not particularly notable previously for its supply of poetic talent.

It seems more likely that these men of ability found themselves in a situation in which a problem was sufficiently dramatized for them to fix their interest in it nearly exclusively. Having fixed upon the problem of poetic creation, they availed themselves of every means of driving the problem to its solution. They allowed their minds to range over much of modern and ancient literature, history, and philosophy, seizing upon what was relevant to their purpose. But, unlike the ordinary person with only a weak sense of his problem, these Fugitives—and Tate in particular—did not merely put trifles in their hoard. Because Tate was convinced of the value of his work and because his Vanderbilt associates kept his critical faculties aware, he left college with some poetry already written and with a supply of knowledge that would enable him to become a critic, a novelist, and a poet.

CHAPTER 2

The Making of a Critic

TATE'S REPUTATION as a critic has always stood high; some would even accord him a greater place as a critic than as a poet. But in an age so much aware of criticism as is the twentieth century, poet and critic are not easily separated. In the Fugitive group, both grew up together. The great merit of the Fugitive discussions was that they allowed the critical to develop along with the poetic faculties. Confronting the full concreteness of new poems in impromptu discussions, these young men acquired the habit of bringing to their materials all their resources. For this reason they avoided becoming theory-ridden: their criticism was naturally forced into taking account of a number of points of view. And it thereby acquired the complexity which must always be the hallmark of good criticism.

When Tate went to New York in 1924, he carried with him the training that would enable him to ask truly fundamental questions about literature. And something of that training was to remain with him and give tone to all his work. For one thing, his criticism has always had an oral quality. Tate assumes the role of the urbane, sophisticated talker, always ready to engage in a polemical discussion, provided he does not have to raise his voice. He carefully disciplines his material, and he uses understatement, irony, and wit as his chief instruments. While he purposely cultivates some resistance in the reader, he never makes it a barrier to understanding.

I *Fugitive Criticism*

For showing the emergence of these characteristics of Tate's later criticism, his essay "One Escape from the Dilemma," published in *The Fugitive* for 1924, is useful. One of three articles forming a discussion of modern poetry among John Crowe Ransom, Donald Davidson, and Tate, Tate's was second in the series, following one by Ransom. In this paper Tate keeps his tones well modulated, moving about his plentiful exhibits of knowledge with a confidence that never requires him to be strident.

Tate's arguments show that his mind is already made up about many of the issues he continued to discuss through the years. He finds himself opposed to Ransom and to Wordsworth in his estimate of the nature of the content of poetry. Tate feels that they both overestimate its rational content, but he defines it as "the pure presentation, of intuitions or ideas."[1] For such a poetry, he declares, there must be an appropriate language. And he finds congenial one of the newest tendencies in versification: that in which the poet is neither completely unrestrained, as were the writers of free verse, nor completely disciplined, as were the traditional writers.

The need for form, Tate says, is rooted in the problems of the time. The modern poet, heir of the skepticism of the nineteenth century, can no longer make use of such concepts as Heaven, Hell, or Duty. He is therefore driven back upon himself because his age has faith only in individualistic intellectualism.[2] Because of this belief, he is interested only in the forms given his material by his own mind. Following such impressionists as Monet, "the modern poet might tell you that his only possible themes are the manifold projections and tangents of his own perception."[3]

So the old analogies of literature with speech and with the desire to make music spontaneously have fallen. Now the poet's utterance has become more difficult and abstract: according to Tate, "it embraces the entire range of consciousness."[4] Now, he says, Baudelaire's theory of correspondences provides a means of controlling this problem; for this reason the theory becomes the backbone of modern poetic diction. He then demonstrates—and here he is following Eliot—that this tradition, though classified as decadent, really belongs with the Elizabethan. All the new poets use the various traditional poetic devices, but they now use them casually. Tate believes that this freedom in the use of convention helps the poet to avoid being a slave to mechanism. The modern poet, in his opinion, simply is making a truly intelligent use of form.

His essay ends soberly, expressing the realization that the modern poet cannot write like Homer or Milton because his experience yields only a "bewildering complexity."[5] Despite the seeming objectivity of his tone, it is hard not to feel that Tate is somewhat concerned about his own position. His concern is a sign of his commitment. Despite the difficulty of the problems of expression in the twentieth century, he is ready to attempt their solution.

II *Literary Reviewer*

Removal to New York in 1924 eventuated in Tate's writing a great many reviews and other essays for magazine publication. His work appeared frequently in *The New Republic* and in *The Nation* and somewhat later in *The Bookman,* in *Hound and Horn,* in the *Sewanee Review,* and in other publications. All of these essays are characterized by a wide sweep of information, acuteness of judgment, and clarity of expression. Taken together, they afford an excellent insight into Tate's concerns during this period. They fall into three broad categories: reviews of literary works, reviews of works on cultural topics, and literary essays.

The clarity and singleness of vision that he had acquired at Vanderbilt is already evident in the early reviews that he wrote soon after his arrival in New York. In "Rhetoric, Mysticism, Poetry," in *The New Republic* for October 14, 1925, he focuses upon three new books of poetry: *Windows of Night* by Charles Williams, *Voices of Stone* by Æ, and *The Pot of Earth* by Archibald MacLeish.

To find a place for Williams and Æ, Tate begins his discussion with an analytical comment on current English poetry. He remarks that Valéry and W. B. Yeats are precisely the kind of poets England has not produced. Instead of major artists, it has had groups of talent gathered together under the designations "wheels," "Georgians," and "Conservationists." The first poet under review, Tate says, belongs to the latter group.

In his criticism of Williams, Tate shows himself thoroughly committed to a modern point of view. He labels Williams "anachronistic" and associates him with the Victorian impulse to didacticism. He feels that Williams is also given to the rhetoric of the Victorians. Citing the Englishman's use of Mnemosyne as an empty personification of memory, Tate shows how Joyce and Proust both "creatively defined her" without ever resorting to empty rhetoric, as Williams has. Set against the full richness of the English tradition, this rhetoric makes Williams ludicrous. And here Tate sets himself firmly, as he does again and again, against the thinness of the mere abstraction in favor of the rich complexity of texture of the concrete.[6]

Tate's juxtaposition of a criticism of Æ with that of Williams works much to the advantage of the former. At least, Tate says, his poetry has the complexity of a full sensibility. The world of Æ, on the other hand, he finds static, proceeding from the poet's mystical vision. His is not like Blake's, which is the kind of mysticism that seeks to unfold an order out of the particularity of experience. Rather, it is like that of Plato, which seeks its mystical order outside the human mind. This disposition makes Æ philosophical in outlook. Yet because his symbolic equipment cannot carry the weight of his emotion, his poetry is cold.

Finally, Tate considers Archibald MacLeish, whose book he describes as one of the best of the year. Tate believes that Mac-Leish is perhaps too dependent for technique on *The Waste Land*: for Tate, the poet shows "an excess of suspended rhythmical periods in long sequences of run-on lines."[7] He believes that MacLeish has observed Eliot's use of Webster and Ford without having gone back to the original authors. But Tate quite approves the experiments with language that he finds in MacLeish. Even though he is guilty of an occasional attenuated metaphor, he will, Tate believes, someday write important poetry.

Tate's review in *The New Republic* of *Poems 1909-1925* would be significant if for no other reason than to examine the nature of his interest in Eliot. But Tate's habit of giving full measure, of trying to bring the artist into focus against his background, makes this review especially important. Though the essay makes clear that the issues he is discussing are brought up for their relevance to Eliot, many of them have quite as much to do with the place of the artist in the modern world.

He begins by making an interpretation of Eliot's turning from America to Europe as a continuation of *The Education of Henry Adams*. Both, he says, represent "a return of the Anglo-French colonial idea to its home."[8] In this process, Eliot has been forced to make himself understand Europe. Tate thinks it significant that Eliot is editing a journal which attempts to relate the

British mind to the total European mind, and especially to Roman culture. Eliot is seeking order in the past, even though the future does not seem to him a strong possibility. By using in his poetry the subject matter of the present crisis of civilization, Eliot gives himself the distinction of making its significance plain, at least in the British Isles.

Tate feels that it has not been generally understood that Eliot is a poet of ideas. His earlier essays, such as "Tradition and the Individual Talent," had expressed confidence in the continuity of culture. But in his later poetry Eliot has steadily anticipated the thesis of "The Function of Criticism": that criticism is "no better than a Sunday park of contending and contentious orators."[9] Now, as a remedy for anarchy, he has proposed a critical dictatorship.

Tate believes that this inclination to a poetry of ideas explains Eliot's development. The idea of spiritual disorder has become for him something protective; it has ceased to be personal. To Tate, his "rationalization of attitude puts in a new light the progressive sterilization of his poetry."[10] Poetry turns into criticism, and Eliot's collected poems begin to seem a mere prelude to a history of European philosophy. His conception is so purely intellectual that it has no symbolic or poetic correspondences. Eliot apprehends reality with the intellect: "This is evidently the formula of *The Waste Land* (1922), where the traditional mythologies are no longer forms of expression, but quite simply an inexplicable burden the meaning of which the vulgar brutality of modern life will not permit the poet to remember."[11] And "The Hollow Men" forms a fitting conclusion to the volume with its "reduction to chaos of a poetry of the idea of chaos."[12]

The foregoing passages are especially interesting because they show a reaction in Tate from his earlier adulation of Eliot. Perhaps these statements can be explained as simple reaction—as the desire to find his own voice. And it seems from today's vantage point that Tate is clearly wrong—that it is precisely Eliot's achievement that he does not reduce his poem to intellectual formulas. One wonders what at this stage Tate understands of the function of Tiresias or how he fails to see the symbolic qualities of the characters which are so brilliantly realized in *The Waste Land*.

But if Tate seems somewhat unappreciative of the symbolic

qualities of Eliot's poetry, he makes up for it in his analysis of Eliot's technical abilities. He discusses two devices, the first derived from Apollinaire: the use of a logically irrelevant but emotionally significant conclusion. The second, which Eliot derived from André Salmon, is the simultaneous projection of events separated in time. This device enables the poet to destroy the common categories of time and space and to produce the illusion of chaos. Tate admits that the influences of Laforgue and Corbière were very great upon Eliot, and the transformation of certain lines from these poets is one of his major poetic devices. But he argues that it is not merely as a borrower that Eliot is a traditional poet. Along with certain other modern poets, Eliot looks upon the Graeco-Roman culture as an organic part of his own. His aim is to use as many as possible of its properties for the benefit of his own age. He does not aim to use the past as such; but, by keeping his attention on the poetry of the past, he aims to give it utility. He defines tradition as life itself; he values it as a living cultural memory. And this helps to make him modern in his outlook, Tate believes.

He concludes by remarking that "The Hollow Men" ends a phase of Eliot's development—the poem may even be the end of what he has to say in poetry. To Tate, Arnold's analysis of Gray is applicable here: Eliot is unable to speak out.[13] If he had come from a different age, he might have had a larger voice.

The review reveals one of the difficulties of the "split sensibility" thesis—its extreme subjectivity. Even though Eliot has come to represent the very type of the artist who thinks through his emotions, Tate finds that he has failed. As this case makes all too plain, emotion and intellect cannot be absolutely separated: there can be only degrees of separation. Perhaps if Tate had not needed so much at this time in his career to declare his independence of Eliot, he might have been more judicious in his appraisal. For he has later expressed many times his highest esteem of Eliot's criticism and poetry.

III *Spengler and the Interpretation of History*

Tate's early review of Spengler's *Decline of the West* makes a significant revelation of some of his ideas about history and causation. Though one would think that Spengler's positivism might be as repellent to Tate as it was to Collingwood,[14] Tate seems to find the German congenial. The young reviewer criticizes the historian for a Procrustean application of his thesis—a favorite metaphor with Tate—but he goes to great length to summarize and explain his thought. Because much of Tate's later work shows his concern with philosophy of history, it is worth looking at some of the ideas from Spengler which he includes in his review.

He begins by comparing Spengler with Hegel, showing how the later historian rejected the dialectic of the philosopher in favor of an interpretation of history as organism. To do so, Spengler returned to Goethe, whose idea of nature as organism enabled him to avoid a split between appearance and reality. Spengler rejected the logic which Hegel had imposed upon life because he felt that it was inconsistent with life.

The part of Spengler's reasoning that seems most attractive to Tate is his demonstration of the opposition between organism and mathematical law. Organism concerns the uniquely occurring event, whereas mechanism supposes the constant possibility of recurrence. With organism, there is growth and decay; with mechanism, the process is reversible. With the latter, history can become whatever the observer wishes: he can tailor history to his own emotions. And Spengler further distinguishes the two systems—the organic and the mechanical—as Time and Space. He says that time in science is reduced to a mathematical dimension; that time is made reversible by mathematical formulae; that this kind of law, entirely spatial, reduces organism to mere causality. Spengler goes back to Kant in making time the form of perceiving and space the form of the perceived. Because every culture must perceive, it must have a way of actualizing time. It does so in accordance with the way in which it actualizes space. The key to the spirituality of a particular culture is the way in which it handles its prime symbol. But here Tate takes issue with Spengler's basic postulate, calling it an example of pure Platonism.

Tate explains that the prime symbol of classical culture is the Extended—Time is corporeality. Time as direction is intolerable, and its actualization as infinite space is consequently denied; hence the notion of space as the Void in Parmenides and Plato. The mathematics of the Greeks was three-dimensional because they had been spiritually conditioned to that number of dimensions. They had a polytheistic religion because they could imagine only a multiplicity of bodies, and they hated the idea of the Infinite or Unextended. But the Unextended is precisely the symbol of modern or Faustian man. It is Time actualized as infinite space; sensuous extension is intolerable to our spirit, and particular bodies are denied; appearances, infinite relations, conceivable only in pure Space, are affirmed. Our metaphysics identifies Reality with Space, the infinitely immaterial—God.

Spengler argues that, when the primary symbol of an age is exhausted, then the civilization of that age must collapse. He feels that the Western World has arrived at such a point. Tate seems to agree with this thesis, and he cites it as another example of a tendency exemplified earlier in Hulme. Like him, Spengler is attempting to replace science with history and is trying to avoid the confusion of mechanism and organism.[15]

These issues which Tate expounds at such length must have appealed to him for their emotional quality as much as for their logical persuasiveness. Like so many other thinkers of the 1920's, Tate is repelled by the excesses so plainly evident in the life of the time. Spengler's gloomy pessimism seems to him entirely justified. And Spengler's interpretation of history was, at base, literary. If he now seems an inverted romantic, this was an interpretation that still had some usefulness in the confused world of the 1920's.

IV *Culture in the Old South*

Along with his reviews of current books, Tate was also writing on more general topics concerning literature and culture. Many of the themes which he expounded during this period are recognizable in his later criticism. The state of letters at a particular time, the relationship of literature and culture, the operation of the past in the present—these are some of the materials with which he has always been concerned.

"Last Days of a Charming Lady" in the *Nation* for October 28, 1925, permitted him to review a question of which he has apparently never tired: the problem of the nature of culture in the Old South, especially as it affected the profession of letters. This essay is especially interesting because it takes a less adulatory tone toward that period than Tate became accustomed to using in the Agrarian controversy of the 1930's. The title itself suggests his opposition to the merely sentimental praise that romantics have so often poured upon that section. Tate finds that the section was never very distinguished for ideas. Worse, its attitude toward the profession of letters was wrong: the older Southerners believed that literature was merely "the product of a charmed idleness."[16] Tate is critical of their failure to recognize the intellectual qualities of literature, and he is impatient with their tendency to be satisfied with the merely physical.

Tate finds the culture of the Old South simply a transplantation of English eighteenth-century ideas. Most of these were only superficially held. A few ideas from the works of Gray and Cowper appeared in the poetry written in the section; a good many knew some of the ideas of Pope; but the works of Scott were of much more importance as repositories of manners. The reason for such a paucity of resources, Tate finds, is that the South lacked a critical faculty. It could not allow criticism to develop because the section was devoted to the perpetuation of its special political idea, and it could not afford to have this idea examined. Because spontaneous self-criticism is the condition that must precede the creation of great literature, the Old South could not write great literature.

Tate's discussion of the religion of the Old South shows the reason for his preoccupation with this theme in his later criticism. The ability to criticize, he asserts, depends upon man's establishment of a relationship with God. Though he does not fully explain his position, he doubtless means that the critical faculty implies some dependable frame of reference. But the Old South had very little to do with religion. It was mostly inclined to support a rigid social order, and with that social order gone, the South has degenerated to mere sentiment.

But Tate is not willing to cast aside everything in the Old South. He believes that the gracious way of life found in Charleston and in Virginia from about 1800 to 1850 was its best feature. And he laments that this society was not so intelligent as it was cultivated, for it might have produced its own Henry James. It is almost impossible not to find here a projection of Tate's own personal interests. As Mrs. Cowan has pointed out, he made many trips with his mother every summer to the old family estate at Fairfax, Virginia.[17] Though he is probably right in finding life in that section gracious for at least a part of the population, he might well have discovered a much less attractive situation in the lives of others in the section.

But he does not force his interpretation upon his readers, and he even goes out of his way to repudiate the sentimentality of mere local color which appeared in the criticism of Edwin Mims. And he tries to fix a true picture of the meaning of the Southern background for literature. The Southerner, Tate feels, having none of the inclinations which come from a more settled religious belief, can approach literature with an open mind. Though he has no culture to depend on, as does the person from New England, this is an advantage. He is forced to become cosmopolitan in order to find himself at all. Both his opportunities and his difficulties stem from the fact that he is a foreigner at home.

V *The Nature of Literature*

Tate's essay "The Revolt Against Literature" is essentially a response to the criticism of I. A. Richards. Tate gives a great deal of attention to the ideas of *Science and Poetry,* but he does not confine himself to a polemical reply to Richards. Instead, he shapes an essay which expresses the condition of modern literature as a function of its historical situation. His basic position has many points of resemblance to those of Hulme and Eliot, but Tate is never the servile imitator. For all three critics the question of tradition in literature is of supreme importance. Tate explains how tradition as a concern of literature showed a marked decline from the time of Sir Philip Sidney to the birth of Wordsworth. Although Tate approves Sidney's cultural approach to this problem, he finds that it had lost its appeal by the time of the eighteenth century. Tate lays the blame on men such as Gibbon and La Mettrie. Because of them and others of like mind, the old Magical View of the world began to fall. And with the destruction of the old myths and beliefs, poetry fell with them. The question of whether or not a new poetry can be restored, despite this absence of belief, is the subject of I. A. Richards' *Science and Poetry.*

Richards believes that he has a solution for this modern problem: though the old faith cannot be restored, modern man can act as if he believes. Tate does not agree; he says that one cannot feel life in a poetry of "pseudo-statement." He believes that a background of assimilated belief is necessary for the creation of any body of poetry. He points out how in Dante the idea and the attitude cannot be distinguished: Dante's intellect and sensibility had not suffered the split which has overtaken modern man. The difficulty of the contemporary poet, Tate believes, is that what he says is asserted with his own sensibility alone, whereas Dante had an ordered system of commonly accepted beliefs. Dante was therefore free to choose his method of presentation in a way impossible for the modern poet.

Tate then explains the pernicious effect of this split between sensibility and intellect upon criticism. Those afflicted with this disease look for the pathology of the artist's ideas instead of examining his works for their artistic qualities. For an illustration, he cites the work of Van Wyck Brooks on Henry James. There the critic studies only the personal in James and misses entirely the point of James's best work. Such criticism, Tate feels, is of the proportion of a menace.[18]

Tate's essay does not give any very satisfactory way out of his dilemma for the modern poet; perhaps there is none. Tate may be closer to Richards than he thinks, for both men essentially are appealing to the imagination. Richards believes that the old symbols can be given new vitality. Undoubtedly his program has some plausibility in that those symbols always implied a certain amount of disbelief as well as belief. On the other hand, Tate implies that becoming emotionally at one with the poetic tradition is required. And for this kind of understanding no quality seems more requisite than that of imagination.

VI *The Condition of American Poetry*

A most valuable kind of essay which Tate wrote during this period was that in which he surveyed the poetry currently being written, put together estimates of individual poets, and made generalizations about the qualities of their poetry. Unusually well-informed, he probably did a good deal to shape the taste of the period. Because he appeared in some of the influential journals, his judgments received the notice of those in a position to count. A representative essay of this kind was "American Poetry since 1920," which appeared in *Bookman* in 1928.

At the beginning of the period under consideration, Tate believes, he can see the end of a popular drive for poetry; this was brought about by the decline of Louis Untermeyer and Amy Lowell. And he sees that Lindsay, Masters, and Sandburg are not truly national poets; they are only capable of *"News from the West."*[19] The Fugitive poets, on the other hand, have not attempted a sectional poetry. Writing simply the best poetry that they could, they found after some years that they were drawing unconsciously on their sectional resources. They showed little interest in public questions but were preoccupied with form and style, interests which had been likewise fostered by Eliot and Pound. Even though Tate is careful to assume a tone of becoming modesty in discussing briefly the history of the Fugitives, he makes it clear that he believes they are setting the true direction for American poetry.

Tate finds the newer poets tending to provincialism, and at this point in the essay he offers estimates of their value. He declares that e. e. cummings "is a deeply moral sensibility without moral ideas" and that this quality "makes him too often the showman." He finds that Robinson Jeffers' "gift for narrative is unequalled in England or America" but that he represents an attempt of the "West to erect its disorder and rootless energy into a symbol of the whole American scene." John Crowe Ransom writes poetry which is "a richly fulfilled moment of vision," but it seems so far incapable of growth and change. Wallace Stevens is "undoubtedly the most finished poet of the age." Of Hart Crane's *White Buildings,* Tate says that it is "probably the most distinguished first book ever issued in the country." Crane has "the most prodigal gift in America"; his "blank verse is one of the few important contributions made by a contemporary to poetic style."[20]

Some of these estimates now seem more enthusiastic than their recipients deserved; Crane, in particular, seems to receive more than his due. And it is doubtful that Tate did full justice to Stevens. Certainly he might at least have mentioned Frost. But the remarkable thing is that so many of his judgments are so nearly those that time seems to be establishing ever more firmly. Quite evidently his critical apparatus, though not perfect, was able to give results that would withstand the changes of fashion.

VII *Evaluation*

The sheer range of interests in all these early essays—and they are of course only a part of Tate's output during this period—suggest a major critic in the making. This is a mind that can never simply assemble a set of dead relationships, but must always be seeking the relevance of its ideas to the problems it encounters. Because it has a focal point, it can encompass a world by expressing the relationship of any particular item to that focus. And it is necessary for him, as for every creature with a point of view, to omit elements which obscure that focus. For Tate, the most important omission is modern science and technology. Perhaps that omission is not so large as it may seem to the casual observer, for he compensates by placing the mind of man in a much larger historical context than does the scientist. If Tate's judgment of value is accepted, then his approach to poetry and to criticism is very nearly definitive.

CHAPTER 3

Tate the Biographer

IN HIS LECTURES on the art of biography, Leon Edel found a symbolic contrast between the desk of the biographer and that of the critic. The former's, he said, must necessarily be cluttered, while the latter's can be clear.[1] If Mr. Edel meant that the critic must have carefully assimilated his material, then perhaps he was right. But since Mr. Edel is a biographer, he probably was simply inflating his own art. His distinction, though inaccurate, illustrates the distance that some suppose separates biographers from other literary men. And for the career of Allen Tate, this suggests a problem: How did Tate—immersed all during the 1920's in the problems of poetry—happen to turn at the end of the decade to biography? And how did he—habituated by now to irony—happen to choose for his first subject a Southern general so frequently romanticized as Stonewall Jackson?

The answers to these questions are necessarily complex. It is quite clear that Tate's first interest in his biographies as well as in his other writings was in the shaping of a literary work. The forms of both his biographies are artistically handled; they contrast sharply with scholarly or journalistic presentations. Instead of primarily providing materials for the reader's own inductions, these books start at points after certain inductions have already been made. Each has its own informing interpretation of the man it seeks to portray; it does not attempt to furnish all the materials for other conflicting interpretations. Its main intent is to be interesting—to present a point of view as the best means of grasping the meaning of character.

I *The Culture of the Old South*

Because Tate believes that men never play out their lives in isolation, he feels the need in *Stonewall Jackson* to explain the culture of the Old South as a key to the mind of his protagonist.

There is no doubt that Tate enjoys giving his ideas about this culture since he feels close to it and since it seems to him interesting in itself. His analysis has a good deal of kinship with some of the ideas of Spengler, whose tone is congenial to Tate. But his ideas also have other overtones, some of which tend to impart a romantic quality to his analysis.

The aspect of society which first comes under scrutiny in *Stonewall Jackson* is economic. In picturing the youth of his hero, Tate feels constrained to show how the ideas of the people of western Virginia became a part of Jackson's intellectual equipment. At that time, money was scarce. But the ownership of physical objects representing wealth was necessary, for in the South of that time a man without such property "did not morally exist." Property and character were equated. A man's public appearance was the whole of his being. Unlike the New Englander, whom Tate describes as "mystical, religious," the Southerner was "practical, materialistic." His wealth had all to be in tangible assets; he points out that "metaphysical wealth," which has been the accepted standard since the Civil War, would have been incomprehensible in such a society. Men of that time valued education, not for itself, but for its possibilities for furthering the acquisition of wealth.[2]

Tate's thesis is open to reservations. Perhaps the greatest difficulty with this picture of economic conditions in the South is that it draws too sharply its distinction between North and South. If the Yankee cultivated the inner life, he also had his share of materialism. At least he managed to acquire some of the more lucrative industries. For example, sixty-nine percent of the cotton manufacture was concentrated in New England as late as 1860.[3] And probably the attitude of the ante-bellum South toward objects of wealth was not so different from that of the present. True enough, the Southerner did not speculate in stocks so frequently as he does today, but his interest in the land was sometimes speculative, just as it is today. Tate's belief that the old Virginia plantation was only productive property to its owners probably oversimplified the facts. And certainly his corollary belief that men of that age thought in space but not in time hardly explains them. If twentieth-century men think in time—and doubtless they do overemphasize time—they are carrying on a tendency long established. Men of Jackson's day also emphasized time, perhaps less than men of the twentieth century, but much more than men of ancient Egypt. It would seem, then, that Tate is exaggerating the differences made in men by their culture.

The most difficult point for the apologist for the Old South is always the problem of slavery, and Tate does not shrink from the problem. According to him, the main reason for Southerners adhering to that institution was that they wished to maintain a stable society. As Calhoun had argued, the chief necessity for the South was not to expand, but to maintain the social order. Within such a framework, the sense of obligation could flourish. If the white man felt some sense of obligation to the Negro, then the latter could have some measure of freedom. But, if he were physically free, he would have been exploited. Northern men did not have this sense of obligation, for they had no sense of a historical, stable society. For this reason they repudiated slavery because it conflicted with abstract morality. But theoretical rightness offered only a poor substitute for the concreteness of moral obligation.

Within this frame of reasoning, Tate's analysis has some plausibility, for he is depending on the conservative's traditional view of an organic principle in society. But when he carries his argument to the extreme of attributing to the Abolitionists the desire "to destroy democracy and civil liberties in America by freeing the slaves,"[4] he certainly does not represent their intentions carefully. To attribute to them a lack of intelligence exhibits mere prejudice. And, too, one wonders at what point Tate believes that slavery could ever have ended.

Later in *Stonewall Jackson*, he makes some analysis of the Civil War as a social phenomenon, and there he shows a decidedly biased point of view. Perhaps the most striking feature of his handling of the subject is what he omitted from his picture. Certainly the Civil War had its unlovely aspects. But there is not a picture in Tate's book of the individual soldier to compare with that seen at Waterloo by Fabrizio in *The Charterhouse of Parma*.[5] The hardships of those who fought for the South are almost legendary; yet Tate shows no more than a generalized picture of such suffering. The gambling on blockade runners and the importation of personal luxuries in certain of the port cities of the Confederacy was shockingly extravagant, yet Tate does not mention them. These omissions tend to reduce his picture of the war to an idealization, hardly recognizable as war.

These interpretations of the underlying social elements in the South give Tate room to stress the freedom of the individual. And it seems as if he is almost purely romantic in emphasizing the possibilities of his hero. For example, he said of the aftermath of First Manassas that if Jackson had been given ten thousand men, he could have ended the war.[6] This, of course, is pure conjecture; if Jackson had had logistical support, if he had succeeded in capturing Lincoln, if the loss of Washington had indeed destroyed the will of the North to fight, perhaps Jackson could have won the war. But war is less a matter of free choice than young Allen Tate thought. The presence of some extraordinary general in Washington, the destruction of a bridge over the Potomac, or a perverse refusal of the North to capitulate might just as easily have rendered Jackson's campaign as futile as the later one of Jubal Early. Certainly much can be accomplished by the exercise of choice; but fortune, then as now, strongly affected the outcome of war.

Tate's overemphasis on freedom of will causes him to make Jefferson Davis the villain of his book. Throughout, Tate makes it seem as if Davis' task were no more difficult than Lincoln's. The incredible accomplishments of Davis in mustering armies, in providing organization to gather supplies, in manufacturing arms (the problem of getting enough raw materials to manufacture gunpowder was itself enough to tax any man's energies), in securing a currency, in appeasing dissident elements within the Confederacy—not to mention the thousands of other grave difficulties he must have encountered—would make one feel that Davis was clearly a man of considerable capability. Few men could have done as well as he did under the circumstances. Yet Tate constantly berates him as if he were a traitor: "From the beginning President Davis didn't want the South to win its own war; he wanted it to act upon a noble and martyred defensive."[7] Tate simply ignores the fact that there were good reasons for fighting a defensive war: the cost of offensive war was more than the South could afford, as the Antietam and Gettysburg campaigns proved. And unless an offensive campaign could have penetrated to the manufacturing and agricultural centers of the North, it might well have been ineffective.

The conclusion to which one would have to come in an examination of Tate's presentation of the society of the South is that it is probably as much a product of the imagination as a statement of conditions as they existed. Probably his error in emphasis arises from his striving to express the uniqueness of the South. Doubtless it did have its uniqueness, but much more emphatically it had its continuity with the nation and with the Western world as a whole.

II *Jackson the Tragic Hero*

As a study in the development of genius, *Stonewall Jackson* shows its greatest strength. Tate gives his book a literary beginning: *in medias res,* at a point at which the character of young Tom Jackson is already beginning to take its form. Already the boy's eyes have their "humorless fixity," which will later be recognized as indicative of an unswerving will.[8] Happily, Tate does no more than hint at the means by which the boy acquired this attribute. It may have come of the adversity of his environment in western Virginia, but Tate leaves it mostly to the accident of genius. Very early in life Jackson developed the power of concentration, which Tate interprets as self-forgetfulness. This quality, as he matured and brought it under control, became "intellectual power of a high order."[9]

While Jackson was at West Point, he began to show evidence of the mental qualities that later distinguished him. He entered the Academy under the great disadvantage of poor preparation. But by sheer application, he was able to remain, though his habits gave him the reputation of an eccentric. Tate feels that this was a mark of his distinction: "character, being the quality that sets a man off from his contemporaries, is not character if it is immediately understood."[10] The clue to his character Tate finds in the quality of his ambition. Instead of seeking a particular object, Jackson simply sought to exercise character for its own sake. Little wonder that such a man would take as his maxim "you may be whatever you resolve to be."[11]

When Jackson found an opportunity to distinguish himself

at Chapultepec during the Mexican War, he no doubt must have felt that his faith in this maxim was entirely justified. But after the war he learned some of its limitations when he became involved in an altercation with his commanding officer while on garrison duty in Florida. Tate barely mentions this episode, so unflattering to Jackson. Perhaps it seems to him an uncharacteristic part of his hero's development, but it is important in that it took him out of the army and into a teaching post at Virginia Military Institute.

Tate explains the ability of Jackson to endure the obscurity of his life as a professor to his having an unusual capacity to rise above circumstances.[12] He could endure both neglect and adulation, as his generalship was later to prove. Perhaps this is another way of saying that in his professorship he learned true humility.

With the beginning of Jackson's service in the Confederate Army, his career took on a kinetic quality. And at this point the book becomes more narrative, less analytical. Jackson is given a series of adversities, a condition for which his religion and his training had admirably suited him. And in this acquisition he becomes a much more dramatic figure.

III *The Making of a Myth*

As Tate interprets this dramatic Jackson, he is one who can resist what seems to be an inevitable fate. The perspective from which Tate describes the battle of First Manassas is one best calculated to point up the opposition out of which Jackson the legend was made. Tate gives the Union Army no clearly delineated qualities except those needful for picturing Necessity. The actual sensory impressions that the men present must have experienced are practically all omitted—sounds, colors, smells. A few props suggest the carnage, but the Yankee Army becomes all movement—first toward Jackson's position, then away as the Union soldiers are met by the fire of his troops. General Bee is the only other character individualized in this particular scene, and he remains only long enough to make his "stonewall" speech.[13]

Jackson himself is brought to the center of the stage and given the role of an Oedipus defying Fate. The subordinate

officers and men of the Stonewall Brigade, though acknowl-
edged, receive roles vastly inferior to that of their general. No
doubt Jackson's qualities are magnificent, but Tate probably
makes the creation of the hero and of his myth much too easy.
The actual events themselves must have been agonizingly
ambiguous. Probably the myth was created because the Confederates desperately needed a hero, just as the darkest days
of 1942 brought forth heroes.

Yet Tate takes his mythical hero seriously. Jackson's wound-
ing at Bull Run is interpreted as a series of histrionic gestures.
He pulls out a "spotless handkerchief" with which to bind his
wound; no hero can afford the realistic grime of battle. His
speech, "It's only a scratch,"[14] sounds more like that of a Boy
Scout than that of a hardened soldier. No doubt Tate was
simply indicating to his audience the fact that he was exhibiting
a hero in action. But he seems unwilling to go much beyond
the conventions, and the result is that this scene has a decidedly
academic quality.

Tate is on stronger ground when he has a larger supply of
fact to support his interpretation. In the next phase of Jackson's
career, his generalship depended upon his understanding the
psychology of his opponent. There he was unquestionably great,
for no one could deny him the glory of such a victory as that
at Second Manassas. Tate describes in excellent detail the
march around Pope's army and the falling upon the enemy from
the rear. And the same generosity of treatment is present in
Tate's account of the engagements at Sharpsburg and at Fred-
ericksburg. The first day at Chancellorsville proves almost the
equal of Second Manassas. But then disaster strikes. Tate does
nothing to subtract from the martyrdom achieved at Chancellorsville, but a Lytton Strachey might well have seen Jackson's
exposure of himself as a desire, unconscious perhaps, for
martyrdom. But it is not part of Tate's intention to deflate
Jackson's reputation.

So Jackson becomes a myth. He is a man whose origins were
in mythic nature: Tate takes pains in his opening chapter to
establish "Let's cross over the river and rest in the shade of
the trees"[15]—Jackson's dying words—as a part of his early
experience. Jackson's mind is permeated with nature. He is un-
contaminated by any breath of industrialism. Likewise, he is

untouched by evil. By omitting the evidence of the seemingly malicious Jackson on his Florida station, Tate keeps his hero clean. True, he has some eccentricities, even occasionally some failures of judgment, but he is never evil.

In this myth are overtones of primitivism, nature worship, and romantic individualism. Jackson is the eternal youth who never had the agonizing ambiguities of maturity to contend with. His occupation required no sordid dealing with money, yet he could make important decisions. If his God was a simple construct, at least he did not doubt Him.

Perhaps what Tate has to say is less important than the form he creates for its presentation. Despite its romantic subject matter, the book has certain almost classic qualities of form. It is a tragedy with a hero struggling against Fate and coming to a certain self-knowledge as a result of his experience. It has a carefully planned beginning, middle, and end. The opening scene is chosen to make an interpretation of Jackson as a person of integrity, determination, and will. The final scene reveals the ironic outcome of his consistent adherence to those qualities in circumstances offered by Fate. The book as a whole represents a careful ordering of experience. And the language itself shows a certain spareness, as if Tate were trying for Hulme's dryness and tightness. By thus imprisoning his romantic hero in classic form and language, Tate at least partially controls what might have been a grossly sentimental work.

IV *Jefferson Davis*

Because Jefferson Davis played the role of villain in *Stonewall Jackson,* he would seem an unlikely candidate for the subject of Tate's next biography, published the following year. But Tate was probably interested in the literary possibilities of the Confederate president's career. If Davis were conceived of as a symbolic figure—the personification of the Confederacy— then his rise and fall might have some of the possibilities of tragedy. Though the quality of its central figure did not fit Aristotle's specifications for the hero of Greek tragedy, perhaps it might have some of the possibilities of an anti-tragedy like *Hedda Gabler.*

The opening scene of *Jefferson Davis* has much more of the quality of drama than *Stonewall Jackson*. Tension is high in this moment of drama, the day of his farewell to the Senate. Mississippi has seceded from the Union, and Davis has made his decision to go with her. Davis himself cannot tell where his decision will take him, but Tate's spectators know that this decision will ultimately bring him only defeat and bitterness.[16]

Tate pictures Davis as a man of destiny, as one who exemplifies in himself the forces that have now reached a climax. In a sense his entire political career has been made of the struggle of North and South. He first came into the public notice because of his part in the Mexican War, itself certainly a part of the sectional rivalry. Then the fates kept him busy in a political career, a large part of which was devoted to the attempts to compromise the sectional difficulties. Now that maneuvering is over, Davis is apparently a free agent ready to choose his destiny. What kind of man is this who is setting about his own destruction?

That he has the Classic weakness of pride is evident from his appearance. About Davis, Tate says, the observer will find an inflexibility of pose; this quality shows itself in the meticulousness of his dress and in the rigidity of his posture. He is a man who shows self-mastery; but, Tate conjectures, he is a man who seems to have conquered an unstable temperament rather than to have brought it into harmony with the other parts of his personality.[17]

The truly essential problem in Davis' character, according to Tate, is the dissociation of his intellect and his sensibility. Tate's application of Eliot's thesis to Davis makes for his most distinctive contribution to the interpretation of the Confederate President. Tate observes of him as he rises to deliver his speech to the Senate:

> One would have supposed that the man could understand people intellectually, by a comparison of their ideas with his own; but not emotionally. He seemed to lack emotional subtlety; while of every logical and intellectual subtlety he was the master. His gaunt ascetic face and withdrawn eyes betrayed a haughty and impatient pride; he would expect ideas to settle the course of events, and not quite grasp the necessity of cajoling men into sharing his desires.[18]

His emotional underdevelopment is grossly evident in his speech to the Senate, and Tate suggests that a detached listener would have been amazed to hear that Davis implies that a better appreciation of the theory of American government would settle the conflict now moving so inexorably forward. But Davis apparently does believe it, and his action upon that belief are fraught with heavy consequences.

Tate sets about the analysis of the early career of Davis to show the origins of this dissociation of his intellect and his sensibility. Unlike the exemplary Jackson, Davis was caught misbehaving at West Point, and he was accused of drinking spirituous liquors at a local tavern. He made his defense upon an intellectual quibble: he pointed out that malt liquor is not spirituous. This surface grasp of the literal problem—a knowing with the intellect instead of an understanding fostered by thinking through the emotions—was all that Davis could grasp of his training at the Academy. His emotional deficiencies meant that he came away with nothing more than "a belief in education as the remedy for all ills, and a haughty pride, an impatience with the imperfections of simple men."[19]

After his graduation from West Point, Davis was blessed with good fortune. But nothing could have been more unfortunate for the development of his character. Unlike Jackson, he had no opportunity, Tate feels, to gain control over his feelings. This ability, the biographer says, "comes by adversity or by long training to a traditional ideal."[20] Because he won his office too easily, he never did "understand that moral and political convictions are the complex product of feeling; for he supposed these to be matters of reason."[21] The man who is addressing the Senate at the secession of Mississippi had been confirmed in this manner of thinking over a period of many years.

Whether or not this picture accurately represented Davis on the eve of his assumption of the presidency of the Confederacy is a moot question. Doubtless it contains some truth, for it does suggest—perhaps somewhat poetically—the condition of all modern men. But Tate's analysis makes this man a pedantic conservative who was unable to move quickly against the North in the early stages of the war. Yet he overlooks the fact that Davis seized the initiative in perhaps as many ways as his resources would allow. Perhaps he acted too hastily. A less truculent attitude at Fort Sumter might well have made it much more difficult for Lincoln to arouse the North. Seizure of Washington for the capital of the Confederacy, as Tate believes might have been desirable, might have brought a quickly negotiated peace, but it might have intensified the reaction produced by Fort Sumter.

As Tate depicts the inexorable forward movement of the war, he finds the early spring of 1862 especially critical for Davis. Before his formal inauguration on February 22, 1862, he heard of the fall of Fort Donelson, and the news made him physically ill. Even at the inaugural festivities, the strain shows upon him. All during the spring he finds himself unable to face both the administrative duties of his office and the social obligations of the evening. He is physically too exhausted to receive visitors. Not only is he under pressure from the Federal armies, but he is being blamed by the Southern press for the Confederate reverses. And so, Tate declares, "he became the solitary Hamlet walking the floor of his study, too proud to fight back openly at his enemies and too frail to bear his responsibility alone without breaking down."[22] Perhaps the comparison is too literary. Davis' problem seems from the vantage point of today to have far less symmetry than Hamlet's. Faced with the incredible complexities of war, Davis may well hesitate. He probably knows all too well the odds against him. If he is indecisive, it is not from over-nicety of discrimination, but from the pressure of circumstance.

But Tate is not willing to find Davis entirely devoid of merit. Perhaps like the hero of Greek tragedy analyzed in the *Poetics*, he needs some saving virtues—something to make the reader think him suitable for the role. And this Tate supplies: whereas Davis seems at the point of complete breakdown early in 1862, he is later able to see and to remedy certain of his shortcomings. The opportunity comes during the crisis over conscription. Although this law is highly distasteful to Davis, he veers round to its support. Of his actions Tate comments: "It is by no means easy for a man to unsettle all his confirmed habits of thought and to strike out vigorously in a new direction; but Davis did this. And the new policy marks him as a great man."[23] Because the new policy is efficacious in producing the large armies used by Lee and Jackson, Davis must be given credit along with them for the victories that make that year the high-water mark of the Confederate armies.

Tate cannot dwell very long on the merits of his anti-hero. In writing of the time which immediately preceded Gettysburg, he finds that Davis is even more subject to his former neurasthenic illnesses: "The strain ... had subtly impaired his capacity to take in the reality around him and to estimate events at their real value."[24] In trying to deal with affairs in the West, he begins more and more to rely on the will of God. Tate feels that Davis is simply unable to make up his mind—he is using God as an excuse to keep from facing his own shortcomings. According to Tate—and surely this contradicts his praise of Davis' stand on conscription—he has learned nothing since about 1843, and he has allowed himself to think by formula. He becomes perplexed by the reverses of 1863, and those who criticize him he calls faithless and unpatriotic.

As the military forces of the Confederacy are thrown back farther and farther, Davis' problems with his generals become more and more acute. His record of appointments has not been entirely bad: the elevation of Lee was his responsibility. His greatest mistake has been the appointment of Braxton Bragg to the command of the armies in the West. Tate describes in detail the military reverses of 1863-1864 in the West, attributing the blame for them in large part to Braxton Bragg. He becomes, in fact, the villain of this part of the biography, and Davis receives the blame for having appointed him and for supporting him. Almost entirely, Tate neglects to give credit to the force opposing the enfeebled Confederates. Against the superb equipment and organization of the Northern armies, there was little that Bragg or Johnston or Davis could do. Yet Tate subjects Davis to this castigation: "In this last year there was in him, perhaps, a little of the madness of pride, a certain tortured resentment against an adversary too complex for him to understand: and yet he felt none of that humility he was later to feel in the face of an incomprehensible Fate. He was now blind Oedipus raging against misfortune, but not yet knowing that he was blind."[25] But he does not give him the stature of an Oedipus, a fact which is painfully evident in the denouement of Davis' career.

Probably because of Tate's lack of sympathy for his subject, the biography of the Confederate president is less satisfactory than that of the general. The difficulty probably lies in the material itself: unfortunately for literary purposes, Davis did not give his life for his country. As a result, his biography must be more shapeless than that of Jackson.

There is some evidence that Tate at this time was also contemplating a biography of Lee. It would have been interesting to see what he might have done with Lee. For it would appear that, in Tate's estimation, Lee stood somewhere between Jackson and Davis. He wrote of him: "He saw everything. He was probably the greatest soldier of all time, but his greatness as a man kept him from being a completely successful soldier."[26] With failings enough to allow the use of Tate's critical faculties, but without enough faults to become a villain, Lee seems almost the perfect biographical figure for Tate.

V *Final Estimate*

Tate's biographies belong with a class fashionable in the 1920's and 1930's—the interpretive biography. By the time that Tate was writing, the type had made a considerable contribution. Especially in the biographies of Lytton Strachey, these works had placed new emphasis on the idea that it is the meaning of a life that must assume first importance. And this school had taught the need for selection as a way of emphasizing that meaning: biography must be something more than an amorphous collection of facts. These writers stressed the importance of detail as the vehicle of meaning. By avoiding the irrelevant, they could emphasize the truly significant, though sometimes minute, elements of the life being presented. All of these qualities are evident in Tate's biographies, and all are used to good purpose.

But the danger of emphasis on interpretation was that it might all too easily be narrow. In the interest of the unified book that would be satisfying to the reason, the biographers frequently simplified human life. In particular, they could shape human motives to the need of the interpretation. All of these limitations have militated against this type of biography so that it no longer holds its former pre-eminence. Though it has left its mark on the art, serious biographers today are less cavalier about departing from facts to interpretation than they were a few years ago.

Tate's biographies have suffered along with the type. And despite their great merits, perhaps they must always have seemed an intrusion on a career seemingly concentrated on poetry. But as signposts in his career, they have the advantage of showing the extent to which he was committed to a literary view of life, to a conservative viewpoint in politics, and to a belief in the need for an integrated sensibility.

CHAPTER 4

Mr. Pope and Other Poems

THE ASTONISHING OUTPOURING of brilliance that marked the beginnings of the Fugitive group resulted in a number of published volumes: John Crowe Ransom had four books by 1927; Donald Davidson, two; Ridley Wills, two; Stanley Johnson, one. Allen Tate, with only a privately printed undergraduate volume to his credit, must have felt the competition. In 1923, while he was teaching in West Virginia, he prepared a volume of poems for publication, but the financial difficulties of his publisher prevented its appearance.[1] Yet it was probably not entirely by accident that Tate delayed in publication. For he was always a severe judge of his own poetry, discarding and revising ruthlessly, sometimes to the dismay of his critics. Very few of his earliest poems seemed to him worthy of republication, but he has admitted that some of his later poems were begun during the 1920's.

In 1928 Tate contributed to the anthology of Fugitive poetry published by Harcourt, Brace and Company. Later that year his own first volume of poetry appeared—*Mr. Pope and Other Poems*. This was a small volume of unusually finished pieces, arranged under the categories of "Space," "Time," and "History." But the poems were too difficult for more than a limited audience, and even the reviewers sometimes seemed to write about them without grasping their meaning.

Yet these poems well repay study. Their combination of traditional form and modern subject matter gives them unusual interest. Perhaps because Tate was aware of his own inner tendency toward romantic exuberance shown sometimes so clearly in his biographies, he gave his poems the tight discipline of some of the traditional stanzaic forms. Following his own prescription in "One Escape from the Dilemma," he loosened these forms with many surprising variations, in the manner of the metaphysical poets. The emotional effect he finally achieved was that contained in an unusual density of subject matter, straining for release from its controlling form.

I "Mr. Pope"

The especial quality of "Mr. Pope"[2] comes from its ability to compress into the smallest space an interpretation of the relationship between the temporal and the immutable in art. Tate chose as his subject a man in whom the personal seemed to be the way to art: Pope's literary quarrels notoriously provided the materials of his satire. Yet out of his personal involvements he was able by some process of objectification to create great poetry. Tate's modern speaker is interested in Pope's procedure, for he, too, is faced with the need to find a way out of his subjectivity.[3] Ironically, though, the poem depends for its effect on its expression of a subjective reaction to this most objective of artists.

The title "Mr. Pope" gives the poem a slightly archaic flavor by reminding the reader of the old-fashioned Southern formality of address—the same quality that Tate was later to stress in "Our Cousin, Mr. Poe."[4] This form of address serves to distance the subject from the reader, while at the same time making Pope comprehensible. For he is thus fixed as a gentleman, with the obligations and rewards of that station. His observer addresses him with a certain deference, and the reader is constrained to follow.

The first stanza introduces Pope, the literary dictator: "When Alexander Pope strolled in the city/Strict was the glint of pearl and gold sedans." So powerful was this man's influence that no matter how casually he went about, the city responded to his presence. The modern speaker notices this condition because he is aware that his city does not respond in like degree to him. The discipline of the imposed order represented in Pope's poetry is implied in the term "strict." But the need for this discipline becomes obvious with the word "glint," which calls attention to a meretricious quality in his society. Though the colors are those of Paradise, their overtones of falseness are a clue to the underlying disorder which gave Pope the need for his emphasis on control. Both Pope's city and the modern city are like Baudelaire's:[5] they are symbolic of hell. It is presumably with a touch of envy that the modern speaker looks on Pope, whose instruments of control had achieved such perfection.

The response of the city to Pope is developed in the picture next presented of the ladies looking out at the poet. They looked out at him—these embodiments of conventionality—with unconscious understanding of the disorder of which they were a part. Instead of pitying Pope as a tragic figure, these women chose the other side of Aristotle's analysis of tragic emotion— they feared him. And they feared him for another reason. Because the sting of Pope's wit disciplined the outcroppings of the disorder underneath their society, they knew that they deserved chastisement. But they had a rationalization available in the thought: "And Pope's tight back was rather a goat's than man's." Pope's back was "tight" because he unconsciously expressed even in his body the control that caused him to use couplets in his verse. But the women could only interpret his back with reference to their own understanding. In their effort to find some system in which to place him, they interpreted everything about Pope as merely personal. They could only see common lechery in the actions by which he expressed his cosmic principle of control.

The transition to the second stanza seems abrupt, but the suppression of the link serves to reduce the distance between Pope the man and Pope the artist: "Often one thinks the urn should have more bones/Than skeletons provide for speedy dust." This observation seems to be provoked by the inability of the women to understand Pope. Essentially, the speaker is questioning the adequacy of the temporal to provide enough for the eternal substance of art, symbolized by the urn. The physical—"speedy dust"—seems to contribute little toward the permanence of art. All kinds of irrelevancies arise in the temporal world to obscure the truth. In reading Pope's poetry, ordinary men take the personal to be the only element of his satire. But, if the content of the urn is the personal Pope, its shape can only be given by the containing vessel.

And the modern speaker, in noting the ephemeral content of the urn, begins to doubt the substantiality of art. The urn has become "hollow" because the objects of Pope's satire have passed away. Inside, it has acquired "cobwebs"—indicative of a determinism that has forced an accumulation of irrelevant content. And even the form of the exterior is obscured by "frivolous rust." These accretions, of course, mean that any trust in the ability of art to speak to all time must be brought into question.

In the next stanza the speaker reaches a climax of bitterness:

> And he who dribbled couplets like a snake
> Coiled to a lithe precision in the sun,
> Is missing. The jar is empty; you may break
> It only to find that Mr. Pope is gone.

Pope is said to have "dribbled couplets," as if they were mere spontaneous issue of form for form's sake. Then he is compared with a snake, which enables the poet to include all at once connotations of time, evil, and terrible beauty. The snake is coiled, for it has assumed the form to which it can shape its material. This form is symmetrical, precise, and deadly—as were Pope's couplets.[6] And the sun, symbolic of reason, helps to show why Pope was so deadly. But no matter how perfectly shaped all of these things were, they now are gone. The deadliness which gave point to Pope's poetry has disappeared. No matter how much the couplets are broken or analyzed, they will not yield the living context in which they were produced.

In the final stanza the Latinate words signal an increased emphasis on the intellectual, which shows the beginning of the narrator's reconciliation to things as they presently exist: "What requisitions of a verity/Prompted the wit and rage between his teeth/One cannot say." The poet wonders what intellectual need provoked the emotional outpouring of art. But the need for truth is not satisfied by its abstractness; truth dwells in the concrete. "Wit" and "rage" both imply their several intellectual and emotional qualities—the speaker combines them to indicate the integrated nature of Pope's sensibility. "Teeth" is a return to the "mineral man"—a reminder of the elemental materials of which man has been shaped. The teeth also are reminders of his kinship with more primitive forms of life; the implication is that Pope's urge to creativity may well have had something to do with the primitive in him as well as the sophisticated.

In the final sentence, "tree" is yet another skeleton: Pope, of course; but it is another reminder of his kinship with nature. Unlike the sequence of events in which the urn must exist, the order of nature provides for the possibility of renewal. The moral which climbs this tree is the type of one of Pope's own sententious generalizations. Though its wording has been obscured by time, it might say as a memorial to Pope that in him is symbolized the condition of all art: the fact that the occasion, the artist, the artwork, and the perceiver are all bound together in an organic relationship. And the speaker hopes that by identifying the moral essence of Pope with the immortality of time in nature, he can himself find a way to the immutable.

II *"Ditty"*

If "Mr. Pope" emphasized Tate's interest in the condition of the artist, this interest was by no means an exclusive one with him at this period. As the categories into which his book was divided would imply, he was actively concerned with all the manifold qualities of the modern mind. For Tate, as for many other modern thinkers, the problem of the nature of the imagination was most pressing. The inroads of science on the modern sensibility, Tate knew, had produced a profound alteration in the ability of man to respond to his surroundings. Against this background of the desiccation of man's emotion, the poem "Ditty"[7] explores the problem of the nature of the imagination of modern man.

The poem begins with a subtle reminder of the effect of time's accumulations upon the imagination. The speaker expresses his awareness of a previous condition, but he does not describe it: "The moon will run all consciences to cover,/Night is now the easy peer of day." This moon, like that of "The Rime of the Ancient Mariner," symbolizes the imagination. But, if the Romantic gave his imagination the softness and passiveness of femininity, modern man cannot quite conceive of this side of his mind in this way. He still finds that the device of personification is a useful aid to understanding. But because he lives in a time which calls for such metaphors of the mind as the Freudian, he necessarily conceives of his imagination as aggressive and even violent. Night, or the unconscious, in this scheme is easily equal to the day, or reason.

The fact that he next finds little boys and cattle aware of this quality of the night is a reminder that nature is no longer what it was to the Romantic. Its reshaping in the consciousness has profoundly altered its effect everywhere. The speaker, following the practice of his spiritual antecedents, goes to unsophisticated creatures to form and to test his understanding of nature. But because the symbols by which the imagination functions have been remade in the modern consciousness, these creatures themselves do not act as if they see nature as the Romantics did.

The second sentence in the first stanza moves abruptly to the speaker's interpretation of the consequence of this remaking of the imagination. This takes the form of an exhortation addressed presumably to modern man:

> Look at the blackbird, the pretty eager swallow,
> The buzzard, and all the birds that sail
> With the smooth essential flow
> Of time through men, who fail.

Instead of looking at nature for the sentimental, vague expansion of imagination, modern man must look at the individual parts of nature. In the concrete, nature can be a reservoir of symbols, each of which can have importance as a focus for the imagination. The speaker illustrates with a bird catalogue, chosen doubtless because the bird was so frequently vaguely and sentimentally used by the Romantics. He includes a "pretty, eager swallow" almost in the form which they would have approved. But he contrasts it with uglier birds of less attractive symbolic qualities. By including the buzzard, the speaker shows how there is also room for evil in his world of spirit. The perdurability of this world of symbols contrasts with that of men, "who fail." The accusing tone of this clause helps this speaker to avoid the sentimental idealization of man of which his Romantic ancestor was guilty.

In the second stanza the speaker becomes much more emphatic. He uses a figure of a drunken man to describe the condition of the imagination in the modern world. Not only does its light not idealize; it positively distorts. It is all-pervasive, penetrating "hill and housetop, street and marketplace." This infection of the lives of men makes them so desperate that they will "plunge" into reckless measures to end this nightmare condition. Their hopelessness is expressed by the numbers rendered powerless by the condition of the modern sensibility. And their arrangement in lines, "mile after mile of men," suggests that they have unconsciously placed themselves so as to obliterate any individual identity. The picture that they make shows all too clearly the determinism that has laid hold of their destiny.

That they are capable of resistance, their attempt "to crush this lucent madness of the face" proves. The violence of this man's expression and the illogical quality of his gesture betoken his inner tensions. Attributing the blame for his condition to the face might seem to involve only externals. The face could be looked on as the receiver of the moon's influence, but it is also the register of the inner condition. Its flexibility allows it to indicate at least the possibility of some freedom of choice. If men had the will, perhaps they could ameliorate their condition.

Yet, the speaker indicates, for remedy they take only a childish course. They go home and "put their heads upon the pillow" instead of seeking an effective remedy. They squirm to stay in the shadow of darkness. In a metaphor that reinforces the emphasis upon their childishness, the narrator observes that they "tuck in their eyes." And their final gesture—sleep—has all the appearance of death. The fact that they are described as "falling leaves" offers some possibility of renewal, but the main stress is one of foreboding for this civilization gripped by madness.

III *"Reflections in an Old House"*

Another poem from the 1928 collection, "Reflections in an Old House," offers a dramatization of the modern mind in its more personal character. The poem is a monologue spoken by a young man whose flair for self-dramatization gives him a Werther-like air. Probably his capacity for genuine feeling is limited, for he has the dissociated sensibility of the modern. He seems to project his feelings into what he sees about him rather than to have emotions that grow organically out of the situation.

He begins his monologue by finding himself an adversary: "When death draws down the blinds in this old house/And

drapes a cobweb through the ante-room,/He will laugh softly."[8]
The gentleness of his personification emphasizes his lack of terror
of death, and it demonstrates his closeness to Romantics like
Whitman. For such a person, death seems to be an opportunity.
Yet the speaker's poise seems unconvincing because of the
limitations he places on the personality of death. His lack of
emotional depth prevents him from comprehending death's
complexity. Even his use of the figure of the cobweb tends to
reinforce this impression; instead of dwelling on its implications
for danger and terror, he conceives it as being all too easily
brushed aside by death's laughter.

Even the mice, symbolic of evil, are never allowed the
insidiousness which might be their primary function. By becoming "thunderous" in the quiet of the house, as the speaker
imagines it will be, they become ludicrous and so lose their
sinister function. Instead of moving by stealth, they "carouse."
And the shadows "mutter gloom" rather than exude it passively.
All of these details which emphasize the momentousness of the
young man's impending death are related by his identification
with the house. But it is an identification quite unlike that in
"Gerontion," for it does not suggest a rich complexity of
experience.

Next, the speaker tries to assess the impact he will have
after death. He first pictures to himself those who will mis-
understand. Some, old and sophisticated, do not look into their
hearts to understand him; instead, they "consult the stars." They
can only say: "Some casual beauty effaced his calendars." It is
ironical that he who was so serious about beauty and who
viewed the passage of time as anything but mechanical should
be interpreted with the devices he most disliked.

Then he conjures up a picture more congenial to his wishes:

> The young ones will stop a moment at the lawn
> Of a withered house, before the incontinent birth
> Of common flowers that nowise different seem—
> That yearly shall take their sweet and golden dream.

This, of course, is what the Romantic wishes for: to be absorbed
into a nature personified—expressed as his own emotional equiva-
lent. The speech that he gives his imaginary young audience

shows that he has achieved the immortality in nature for which he longed.

But this mood does not last: good Romantic that he is, his pain is never far from his joy. His young audience will not really understand, he says, because "None will recall, not knowing, the twisted roads/Where the mind wanders and the heart corrodes." These are the tones of the Byronic hero, whose search for fullness of experience, whose satiation with that experience, and whose final disillusionment must all be misunderstood by ordinary men.

The final stanza of the poem returns to the scene of Death in the old house. He is making a grand exit. What he has left behind is

> . . . an unenvisaged hint
> Of a young man who, in a stormy drought,
> Rebuilt these fields in a slender Septuagint,
> Translating our uncollected interest
> Of the sun buried in a winter's West.

Unashamed egotist that he is, the young man does not minimize his hardship, for he needs adversity to prove his individuality. But the extreme of his unconscious irony is reached in his implied comparison of his own inspiration with that of Moses. The fact that he qualifies his description of his book with the adjective "slender," or that he speaks of himself as a translator, does not really reduce his estimate of himself. The final impression in this presentation of the Romantic mind is that of an ego so tremendous that it does not scruple to compare itself with God.

The little poem "To a Romanticist"[9] immediately followed in the 1928 volume. Later it was called "To a Romantic" and had the date 1924 and "To Robert Penn Warren" added. The effect of these additions was to give the poem a personal quality and to allow it to stand alone as a bit of youthful mockery. But its place in *Mr. Pope and Other Poems* seems to make it a commentary on "Ditty," its predecessor in the book.

The speaker's tone in "To a Romanticist" shows kindly appreciation of the young man's enthusiasm, but the older man also feels the need to issue a warning. By holding his "eager head/Too high in the air," the young man succeeds in avoiding the experience of the dead. This reminder to the young man of "Reflections in an Old House" is appropriate, for he has shown himself interested in having his own death mean something to future generations, though he has not shown an equal interest in learning from those who might have instructed him. The speaker calls the dead "sleepy" because he wishes to remind the romanticist of their continuing influence. But the dead are represented as those who have become bored with the elevated tone of romantic talk of symbols and self.

The lines "Your head, so turned, turns eyes/To lose in a vagrant West" contain an intentional ambiguity. The romanticist's head is "turned" both in the sense that he is egotistical and that he chooses to impose a limited point of view on his experience. He inflates the objects of his interest: he says "sublimest talk" and "vehement house." And these expressions are intentionally parodied in the speaker's "vagrant West." Emphasizing his ironical view of the romanticist's inflation of the future, he then compares him with Ozymandias.

The speaker accuses the romanticist of interpreting the dead according to his own wish. Because he himself wants to be idealized after death, he thinks "the dead arise/Westward and fabulous." Against this expansive picture, the speaker ironically juxtaposes one which expresses the evil nature of man and the limitations of his destiny: "The dead are those whose lies/ Were doors to a narrow house."

This figure of the grave as a house brings to mind its use by Emily Dickinson. Tate has sharpened its ironic quality by contrasting it with the house of his first stanza. But in so doing, he only makes explicit the need for controlling the romantic impulse not far underlying the modern sensibility. Tate's speaker seems to feel the need for curbing this romantic expansiveness more than did Miss Dickinson's. Perhaps the pressure of ideas on the world-view accounts for the difference: the twentieth century was beginning to find more danger in romantic ideas than had the nineteenth.

IV "Ignis Fatuus"

In "Ignis Fatuus" Tate dramatizes the intensity of the yearning for intellectual experience in modern man. For this purpose he chooses a speaker who has mental qualities not far removed from those of the romantic of "Reflections in an Old House." But if he has envisaged man's possibilities, he is no longer able to believe completely in them. For this reason, he makes his treatment ironical, as his title announces.[10]

The exploration of the tones in which the speaker comprehends his problem gives Tate an opportunity for a dramatic presentation. The poem is a monologue addressed by one side of the speaker's mind—his normal reasoning self—to his emotional self, which might be called his *anima*. It is evident that the speaker is suffering from the dissociation of his sensibility from his intellect and that he is making an effort to recover what he recognizes he has lost.

Although the title of the poem has given a hint of the ironical quality of the speaker's mind, he begins without showing much of that quality: "In the twilight of my audacity/I saw you leave the world. The burnt highways/Of summer gave up their light." The light imagery, which is dominant in the poem, helps to clarify "audacity." Though this abstraction bears some of the connotations of pride, its context brings out some of its nobler associations. It is especially important that the twilight softens and absorbs the harshness of the determinism symbolized by the highways and the intensity of the unrelieved reason suggested by summer. Modern man's preoccupation with this side of his mind, the speaker is saying, needs to be expanded by the emotions which culminate in the imagination. But the speaker must follow reason with "fear-disbursed eyes." Lacking any complete integration of sensibility and intellect, he cannot be sure of his identity and is painfully unable to act.

In the second stanza he describes his efforts:

> Towards the dark, which harries the tracks
> Of dawn, I pursued you only. I fell
> Companionless. The seething stacks
> Of corn-stalks, the rat-pillaged meadow
> Censured the lunar interior of the night.

The dark implies chaos; the speaker is willing to risk the disintegration of personality which, as Tate has implied,[11] lurks always behind the modern consciousness. But the speaker keeps his attention on the dawn: the feminine, imaginative, creative side of his personality. Because his is not a creative society, he has been driven into a sterile individualism. The result of this condition is not only alienation from his companions but from nature as well. Instead of the soft personifications of nature available to a Wordsworth or a Whitman, he can only perceive a perverted nature. The phallic symbols of the cornstalks and the dirty sexuality of the rat show the kinship of his interpretation with that of *The Waste Land*. This nature has "censured" the mind because nature is a projection of that mind; the externals are simply an indication of the "lunar interior"—a derangement which indicates a perversion of the imagination.

In the third stanza the poem turns on the question, "High in what hills, by what illuminations/Are you intelligible?" The "hills" of this question suggest the imaginative expansion of mind needed by him and his age. The word "illuminations," with which he continues the light figure, hints at an outside source of light. "Intelligible" implies a complexity that must be resolved. Altogether, the question presents the need for the integration of the sensibility and the intellect.

The sentence which follows does not answer the question; it attempts instead to illuminate the problem by expanding it: "Your fierce latinity/Beyond the nubian bulwark of the sea/ Sustains the immaculate sight." "Latinity" and "nubian" bring to mind not only emotional associations with distant places, but intellectual ones as well. History, anthropology, philosophy—all are by implication part of his vision. And the word "immaculate" adds a religious quality as well.

What he has envisaged makes his return to his waste land entirely disillusioning: "To the green tissue of the subterranean/ Worm I have come back." "Green" is here used for its power of multiple suggestion, much as in Marvell's "Garden." Primarily it hints at the possibility of renewal, but it also contrasts with the idea of autumn and death in the figure of the corn stalks of the second stanza. The noun that it modifies, "tissue," refers not only to the animal, but it helps to establish the kinship of man with all the world of nature. Yet in a modifying phrase he shows the possibilities of ambivalence in this world of nature. If "green" suggests the healthy potential of renewal, the subterranean worm shows how nature is also permeated with insidiousness and evil. The worm is akin to the serpent in Eden, and the man's return to it indicates the imperfection of his nature. This lack of perfection, no doubt, is the reason he has been unable to achieve his quest.

The final question is cast in a form that brings together the issues relevant to this experience: "Where is the riot/When the pigeon moults his ease/Or exile utters the creed of memory?" Tate later changed the "riot" of the early version to "light," thereby improving the unity of the poem. But the first version had the advantage of hinting at the theme of the disintegration of personality. And the second version seems much more pessimistic.

The pigeon, the dove sacred to Venus, is therefore symbolic of the spirit of love. But "moults" undercuts the element of idealism by emphasizing the earthy. The speaker's loss of the spiritual and his return to ordinary reality may not be the only solution, however. Perhaps the gap may be bridged in the "creed of memory." The memory itself is a means of integration; and by describing it in religious terms, the speaker implies the order of dedication necessary for the process of integration.

The poem emerges, then, as a metaphor of the spiritual condition of twentieth-century man. Its greatest contribution is its tone—slightly bitter, but intellectually controlled. The speaker, fully aware, is not crushed by his condition, but neither is he indifferent. The very fact that he is able to focus and control the picture of his condition is a subtle reminder of the possibility that the sensibility and the intellect can be united and integration achieved.

V *Conclusion*

Tate's contribution in his 1928 volume was that he gave form to a part of the poetic sensibility of the twentieth century. Though all his writing shows an evident desire to comprehend this sensibility, he was too sophisticated to attempt a definition. By comparison with a writer such as Whitman, who was always ready with generalizations about the place of poetry in his age, Tate seems singularly modest. Each poem is in its way a metaphor—implicit rather than explicit—of the sensibility of the age.

His method is somewhat an outgrowth of his understanding of modern man's reliance upon scientific determinism. He seems to interpret the mood of the twentieth century as made up of both an emotional and an intellectual awareness of a bewildering complexity. The old simplifications had been falling for a long time when the twentieth century began—at least since the Renaissance. But the speed of their fall had vastly accelerated in the nineteenth century. The old geology, the old biology, the old physics were supplanted by new, abstruse sciences beyond the comprehension of the layman. Along with these sciences moved others closer to man himself: the new anthropology, sociology, and psychology all contributed to an interpretation of the nature of man which made him far more complex than he had seemed before. Man—always something of a mystery to himself—became even more a source of bewilderment to himself; and the possibility of genuine self-knowledge seemed ever more remote.

Doubtlessly, the horrors of World War I revealed to man a side of his nature not fully realized before. Perhaps most of the writing of the 1920's had upon it the marks of that struggle. Tate did not concentrate upon it, but he, too, must have suspected that man's nature was not so susceptible of control as it obviously needed to be. The search for self-knowledge that he dramatized in his poems has about it an urgency that effectively suggests the abyss that his generation had seen before their feet. This urgency shows itself in the discipline which Tate asserted over his material. It is this ability to incorporate the tone of his age into the rhythms of his poetry that made his work so promising for the future.

CHAPTER 5

Agrarianism

THE PUBLICATION of *I'll Take My Stand* in 1930 brought Tate and the eleven other Southerners who participated in the anthology into popular notice as "Agrarians." The title of their book seemed to announce a militant sectionalism, but this attitude was not borne out in the essays themselves. The title seems to have been the publisher's idea; Tate liked it so little that he disclaimed it in a footnote.[1] The organization of the book was simple: it began with a statement of principles, followed by essays on subjects such as John Crowe Ransom's "Reconstructed but Unregenerate," Donald Davidson's "A Mirror for Artists," Frank Owsley's "The Irrepressible Conflict," and Stark Young's "Not in Memoriam, but in Defense." Although the book went contrary to the leftist tendencies then fashionable, it had impact enough to call for two more anthologies: *Culture in the South* (1934) and *Who Owns America?* (1936). Obviously these books have not done much to shape social legislation since that time, but they had importance for the cogency of their criticism of the existing order and for their intellectual and esthetic program.

A compact summary of the ideas of the Agrarians is contained in the "Statement of Principles," which forms the introduction to *I'll Take My Stand*. The authors announce themselves as Southerners, and they express a preference for the Southern way of life as opposed to the American. They feel that this attitude can best be summarized in the phrase "Agrarian versus Industrial." The Agrarians believe that industrialism means simply the decision of society to invest its capital in science. Their examination of the history of this commitment forces them to conclude that this investment has yielded the laborer small benefit. Hard work and insecurity are his lot, not happiness; and the Agrarians feel it obvious that men should be able to enjoy their work. Other evils that have followed the machines are overproduction and unequal distribution of wealth. The habit of hurry incidental to work in an industrial society has insinuated itself even into the workers' moments of rest so that they scarcely can refresh themselves in the time allotted for rest. In an industrial society, the Agrarians aver, nature becomes a mere group of usable commodities. But nature should be for man something more complex—something "mysterious and contingent."[2] The loss of this quality causes the sensibility to decay. Religion and the arts—both of which are founded on the right relation of man and nature—suffer.

The Agrarians believe that reform which requires compromise with industrialism is impossible. Even the Humanists cannot offer a workable solution to the problem of machines and society because their ideas are too abstract. For the Agrarians, the true pattern of reform lies in the direction of the genuine humanism of the older South. But they are somewhat doubtful of attempting overt political action. They want simply to point to their belief that "culture of the soil is the best and most sensitive of vocations."[3] Perhaps the Democratic party can be brought over to agrarianism; perhaps another will be needed. But only the cowardly would say that it is impossible to throw off the evil of industrialism.

The Agrarians do not profess to think that their ideas are new; in fact, they probably have espoused them because they are not new. Undoubtedly their Classical education had much to do with the form their ideas took: their intellectual antecedents certainly went back to Horace and perhaps Hesiod. And in America, there was Thomas Jefferson, who thought that the New World should remain agricultural so as to avoid the problems of the rabble of the cities of Europe.[4] Still another source of their ideas was the Romantic stress on Nature "that never did betray the heart that loved her"—a belief that aligns them with popular American ideas about life in the country. And primitivism, with its search for people unspoiled in a state of nature, has long been evident in much of American literary and social history. Each of these ideas must have contributed to the climate of opinion in which Agrarianism developed.

But it is also tempting to look upon Agrarianism as an extension of some of the ideas about agriculture which came into prominence during the latter part of the nineteenth and early part of the twentieth centuries. During those years the farmer had gone through a series of agricultural depressions, and agitation about his plight had echoed in the national political campaigns of many of those years. Populism had had a strong impact in the last decade of the nineteenth century, and Bryan had mobilized agricultural interests in his "Free Silver" campaigns. The South had been much affected by this agitation, as was shown in the campaigns of Tillman of South Carolina and Tom Watson of Georgia. Though the farmer did not have power enough to win many political campaigns, his agitation did perhaps help to establish him as a symbol of an embattled and virtuous advocate of a decent way of life.[5]

And the farmer, from a symbolic point of view, was fortunate in his enemy. The industrialism of the nineteenth century could hardly have been more hideous. Dominated by rapacious management and unrestrained by government, industrialism came to be associated with all that was inhuman. For many, like Frank Norris' Shelgrim in *The Octopus,* the machine itself, symbolic of determinism, was at fault.[6] Instead of blaming the directing intelligence behind the mechanism, he and many others like him tended to attribute the fault to mechanism itself by personifying the machine.

Unlikely as it seems, Tate himself eventually tried an essay on economics. Though he was not a specialist in that discipline, he had the intelligence to work with its symbolic and human aspects. He was, therefore, not so unlikely a writer on the subject at it might seem. His "Notes on Liberty and Property," published in *Who Owns America?*, does not pretend to factual exhaustiveness; it is rather a polemical treatise designed to keep before its readers a strongly Agrarian thesis.

The essay emphasizes the effective control of property as opposed to its mere ownership. The layman's belief that ownership means control is, he says, false. Property rights are always relative, and the extent to which an individual or a group can control its property is the extent to which it has liberty. To demonstrate the inability of certain property owners to control what they own, he cites the case of a stockholder in the United

States Steel Corporation. He has only the rights of collecting the dividend and of selling the stock. Because the stockholder cannot control the policy of the corporation, Tate feels that he has no effective ownership. He points out how a similar situation prevails in the collectivist state: its citizens may have security, but they have no freedom because they have no control.[7]

The second section of the essay develops the reason for the small property owner's misapprehension about the nature of property. Big business has played upon his inability to differentiate between kinds of property. This incapacity of the average man leads him to identify his own interests with those of the great corporation. He must be taught, Tate says, the difference between tangible property, which is controlled by its owner, and corporate property, which is controlled by a clique.

Economic liberty, according to Tate, is the power to choose between selling and using. He demonstrates how much more effective is the farmer's ownership of a hog than is a stockholder's ownership in a tire corporation. The farmer can eat the hog, but the stockholder cannot control the market for tires; and he cannot use up enough tires to keep even his share of the corporation going. Tate declares that agriculture also makes people more responsible than any other form of social organization, for it forces men to exercise control. Because the stockholder has no control, he develops no responsibility. And because the corporation necessarily produces for the market, it must regard labor as a commodity to be used in meeting the market. It therefore deprives its management as well as its stockholders of social responsibility.

For those who feel it inevitable that corporations should flourish, Tate has small sympathy. He says that the power of giant corporations comes solely from the will of those who wish them to have power. For those who argue that the corporations, despite their faults, are necessary to produce large amounts of wealth, he points out that a nation can be very rich collectively while allowing large numbers of its people to remain poor. But the remedy, he feels, is not complete obliteration of the corporation. Rather, it should be the reduction of centralization. The nearer a society comes to personal production for personal use, the freer it is, Tate believes. A complete return to this form of production is now impossible, but society should emphasize as far as possible individual ownership and control.[8]

Many of Tate's ideas are obviously not original. His attack on the size of the corporation without sufficient evaluation of its social function merely revives the thinking of some of the early Progressives. Much of what he has to say about the farmer's advantage is simply a misunderstanding. He minimizes the imperative need for efficient production and marketing in both farm and factory. In his overemphasis on the economic freedom of the individual, he comes perilously close to sentimentalizing the farmer. He probably had not felt the experience of farming as Hawthorne did at Brook Farm.

But it would not be fair to judge Tate's part in the Agrarian movement solely on what he wrote about economics. A more important essay was his "Remarks on the Southern Religion" published in the original Agrarian anthology in 1930. This paper has a literary quality: basically, it is the elaboration of a figure. To describe what he means by religion, he employs the metaphor of a horse. Modern religion, he says, is interested only in the part of the horse represented by its analogy with the machine. His religion teaches a belief in omnipotent human rationality; paradoxically, he holds this belief as an irrational article of faith. This half-religion enables its communicants to see only what they wish to see; by holding it, they can believe in the ultimate success of all their endeavors. But the religion of the whole horse—which takes into account the horse as organism as well as mechanism—can predict failure as well as success. It takes into account the evil which marks every human being. Because it is a mature religion, it is not likely to suffer collapse.[9]

In order to relate the religion of the South to this religion of the whole horse, Tate turns to the ideas of history by which that religion must be interpreted. On the one hand, he finds history as image; on the other, history as idea. In the latter view, history becomes a series of abstractions: Greece and Rome are not differentiated. This is the Long View, and it is closely allied with the religion of the half horse of modern man. The Short View, on the other hand, makes history temporal and concrete. For it, history is the specific account of the doings of specific men. Men are thereby placed in the fullness of their complex and contemporary settings. For Tate this fact renders their motives believable.

The Long View is the way of abstraction. It removes the element of uncertainty—of accident or contingency—because it simplifies the past so radically. It emphasizes the likeness between the elements in a temporal series and so removes all concreteness from the past. In the Long View, religion suffers badly. Christianity is reduced to a vegetation rite, and there is little to choose between it and the cult of Adonis. Because Tate is opposed to this simplification, he says that the destruction of the uniqueness of Christ in this Long View means that He is entirely obliterated. This is the death of Tradition. But the particular problem of the Western mind is how to keep its tradition operative, for it must be automatic in order to remain tradition.

He then makes an analysis of the quality of the European mind which has led to the present problem. He says that it was "both a great discovery and a great calamity" when Europeans discovered that reason could be used to defend the irrational. Scholasticism tried to make rational all the symbols and myths of religion, but the men of the Renaissance went even further. They advocated that all the part of religion which could not be made to work should be discarded. The medieval church had restrained this practical side of its members by its stress on the fundamentally evil quality of nature. It forbade its members to have anything to do with this nature, but such a prohibition is always likely to incite revolt. When men overthrew the medieval dispensation and the myth of nature was destroyed, nature became merely logical and practical.[10]

Tate finds that in religion America is entirely continuous with Europe. This phenomenon accounts for the fact that the Old South had a feudal society. The section's conservatism caused it to retain the feudalism of its beginnings, but it did not at the same time create an appropriate religion. This confusion in the South's point of view prevented it from separating soon enough from the North to be able to save its institutions. And the lack of an appropriate religion today is causing the present breakdown in the social structure of the South.

But if the South had no appropriate religion, at least it took the Short View of history. New England went over to the Long View during the nineteenth century. Because the section relied so heavily on abstractions, it had no sensibility of its own; it substituted a parasitic dependence on the emotional life of

Europe. The result was that New England became a "vast museum."

The South, on the other hand, had no need to give itself European airs because it was Europe. The South did not need excessive learning because it did not need to put up an appearance for the vulgar. Its mind functioned by images rather than by abstractions. Because its people did not need a rigidly undeviating line of logic to make their connection with the past, they could combine such unlikely elements as the biblical, the Greek, and the Romantic. Living by the concrete image, they did no unnecessary work and acquired no unnecessary knowledge. They used their history simply to see in it an image of themselves.[11]

But the South broke down partly because its life did not admit of a right mythology. The South, Tate reiterates, would never have collapsed if it had had a religion suitable for its kind of life. To the question of how the Southerner can now get back into his tradition, Tate's answer is "by violence." A reactionary political program is the most violent of all reforms, but this is the only possibility for the present-day Southerner.[12]

The thesis of this essay makes one of the most interesting interpretations that Tate ever advanced; it forms the core of an interpretation of the Old South that might well be expanded. The question of how far people can live by abstraction as opposed to the concrete is indeed fundamental. Tate's argument about the Old South seems plausible; the section does not seem to have lived very much by abstraction.

But he could not have lived entirely in the concrete without some abstractions to classify his thought for interpretation. His failure to stress the system of organizing the content of the Southerner's concrete images leaves the possibility that they might have been merely chaotic. Perhaps Tate needs to explain whatever sub-verbal form of organization he may have conceived to account for the way in which the Southerner's images were classified and thereby permitted to yield meaning.

How is one to know the society which lives fruitfully by images and one which merely passively allows its images to go through its mind without comprehension? By any test that it seems possible to devise, the Old South did not measure up particularly well. An exception might be made for the political thought of Virginia during the Revolution and afterward. But the North also produced its share as well. If one looks at the literary output of the section, it is very difficult to see that the South was at all the equal of New England. In music, in art, and even in architecture, the South was only modestly creative.

This lack of substantial proof of the values of Agrarianism as a way of life is the great criticism of Tate's venture into economic and political philosophy. It is a little difficult to believe that he was not doing what many others still do—sentimentalizing life on the farm. However damaging this excursion may be to Tate's standing as a political thinker, it does not do him comparable damage as a poet. For as Eliot remarked, one does not demand an original philosophy of a poet. Perhaps it might even be an impediment. What is important about this part of his career is Tate's ability to find in it material about which he could feel intensely. For his function as a poet required not so much that he provide answers as that he ask questions—and not so much that he express logical arguments as form the sensibility. Happily, Tate's venture into political economy was only a digression, and he was soon back at his true business of writing poetry.

CHAPTER 6

Selected Poems (1937)

DESPITE HIS DIGRESSION into Agrarian activities, Tate continued to put a great deal of his energy into poetry. He published volumes in 1930, 1932, and 1936, and his poems appeared frequently in the periodicals. Not the least of his effort went into the culling out of poems he thought unfit and into the revision of poems already published. Critics like Louis Untermeyer felt that Tate was destroying his original creative impulse in so much revision, and the poet took notice of them in his preface to the 1937 volume.

He begins his essays by remarking that he has rejected for this collection more than half of the poems that he had included in *Mr. Pope and Other Poems*. He mentions his inclusion of most of the poems of the 1932 volume and all of those in *The Mediterranean and Other Poems*. "Sonnets of the Blood," he points out, has been almost completely changed from its original version in *Poetry*. And he describes how "Ode to the Confederate Dead" was completed only after ten years of labor that had even included the help of other poets. Finally, he is seeking an answer to his romantic critics who feel that his poems cannot have integrity except within the unity of his own spontaneous poetic consciousness. His answer is that his concern as a poet is not with his own experience but with that of those who read his poetry. Because this emphasis requires that he put his stress on the achieved form of the poem, he can dismiss the intricacies of the problems of poetic psychology. It is probably no accident that he provides in this volume one of the best illustrations of his ability to find through much experimentation a perfect controlling form in his "Ode to the Confederate Dead."

I   *"Ode to the Confederate Dead"*

In any survey of Tate's work, it is impossible to ignore the "Ode to the Confederate Dead." The analyses of Tate himself and of his critics have established it as the best known of his works. But they have also tended to render additional criticism difficult. After a brilliant critic like Tate has written on his own poem, what more is one to say? He himself perhaps provides the answer in his discussion of the relationship of the author and his reader: " . . . as a poet, my concern is the experience I hope the reader will have in reading the poem."[1] Each reading, in this view, must have its moment, however brief, of illumination. Tate's essay on his own poem need not be regarded as having done any more than what an extraordinarily gifted critic could do. There must always remain room for another point of view.

A technique of which Tate made relatively little use in "Narcissus as Narcissus" is the comparative study of earlier and later versions of the poem. As a poet, he would naturally wish to stress the final form of his expression, and it would be only natural to avoid or even to suppress earlier versions of the poem. Certainly any judgment on the poem should be made on the author's final choice of expression. But when the earlier version help to illuminate the later one, it would seem to make a valuable adjunct for the reader.

Even small changes in a poem like "Ode to the Confederate Dead" are likely to be quite significant because all versions of the poem are focused through the mind of a perceiving consciousness. What the man in the poem says is always a part of a much larger and more complex entity—the whole mind of the man himself. And his mind in turn is a small indicator of a much larger and still more complex entity—the mind of man in the twentieth century. And this mind itself is only a part of the mind of mankind. For these reasons, the displacement of a phrase has much larger implications than might appear at first sight—so large, in fact, that probably no one could see far enough to encompass them all. It was no false modesty that led Tate to declare that he felt the poem beyond his powers; it is literally beyond the powers of any man. And this, of course, is its fascination.

As he himself points out, this poem is about solipsism:[2] the belief that the individual creates the world in perceiving it. The need for such an outlook is perhaps derived from the problem of the locked-in ego of modern man, a theme which Tate would have found "in the air," though one notably emphasized in the final section of *The Waste Land.* In the "Ode to the Confederate Dead," Tate dramatizes this problem by presenting the feelings of a modern man who is being forced to face his essential isolation. This Tate accomplishes by having him encounter a set of symbols, the chief of which is a Confederate cemetery. There follows a record of the stream-of-consciousness which ensues, proceeding from initial quietness through rising intensity to a climax, and finally ending in a denouement expressing his acceptance of his modern condition. The advantage of this arrangement is that it frees the utterance for a presentation of the full emotional-logical complexity of the man's situation. Being thus free, the utterance demands the facing of all the complexities inherent in each of the symbols. The content of the poem, therefore, is enormous—so great that no single reading could encompass it all.

The title in the earliest versions of the "Ode to the Confederate Dead" is amplified by the dates "1861-1865," which appear immediately beneath.[3] This device, though apparently insignificant, hints of a stronger tendency to memorialize the dead Confederates than in the later version of the poem. This would seem to give the man at the Confederate graves a stronger reason for his solipsistic contemplation than later seemed necessary. The speaker in the final version of the poem, being markedly more philosophical than his earlier counterpart, does not need to live by his impulses as much as a man who has not reflected on his experience.

In the second line of the earlier version, the headstones are said to "barter their names to the element," instead of the later "yield."[4] The use of a figure from trade implies that the speaker is a man of action. But unfortunately a long meditation does not seem particularly appropriate to such a man. Meditation for him might seem sentimental and insincere. Perhaps he would not be self-conscious enough to be concerned much with the problem of identity. For all of these reasons, Tate's changes make a considerable improvement.

The speaker's outlook on nature provides one of the most important means of indicating the quality of his mind. Like the Romantics, he relies on personification. Unlike them, he seasons his expression with figures expressive of mechanism: "The wind whirrs without recollection." The balance between these two sides of the speaker's mind came in for considerable attention in the process of revision. In the original version, nature's "sacrament" was opposed to the "sinkage" of death. The figure is much more mechanical than the final one of the "seasonal eternity of death." Much the same kind of change transformed the earlier "their business in the vast breath." That speaker could only interpret nature in the vocabulary of commerce. In the later poem a personification of heaven suggests the range of the speaker's comprehension. But his expression is ambiguous enough to allow for the doubts of modern man in his search for a controlling principle in the universe.

In the second section of the poem, the later version adds the two lines, "From the inexhaustible bodies that are not/Dead, but feed the grass row after rich row." The speaker's meditation concerns the inability of man's physical being to resist the effect of time. All the men in the cemetery are lying there without individual identities: they are merely "memories" of mass actions. Their present identities are merged in the concept "Confederate"; and this identification is interesting to the observer because he, too, is merged in some such grouping of men. The added lines may seem to avoid this problem and to express a romantic individualism like that of Whitman. But paradoxically, they say perhaps what they least expect to say: that the speaker fears that the bodies are capable of being exhausted. They are part indeed of the circular process of nature, but in its operation individual identity is eventually obliterated. With this change in the original context, the antagonism expressed in the second section between time personified in "November" and the idealization of mankind in the stone angels becomes more comprehensible. Time is conceived of as freedom of opportunity as opposed to the determinism of idealization. The speaker implies that the fixity of the idealization, the overstressing of the purely rational is at the heart of the spiritual illness of modern man.

Both versions of the poem agree in their stress on the ability of the idealization to drive the individual back upon his primitive impulses, symbolized by the crab. But the emphasis in the later version is stronger:

> The brute curiosity of an angel's stare
> Turns you, like them, to stone,
> Transforms the heaving air
> Till plunged to a heavier world below
> You shift your sea-space blindly
> Heaving, turning like the blind crab.

Whereas the earlier speaker was passive and unresisting, the later uses figures of motion. The heaving and turning are primitive and apparently futile, but they give the perceiver at least the benefit of some action. Yet his identification with the crab proclaims his awareness of the limitations upon the man of "locked-in ego."

The refrain which follows the second section is the first of four added at the suggestion of Hart Crane. It lends emphasis to the Whitmanesque interpretation of the leaves as individuals: "Dazed by the wind, only the wind/The leaves flying, plunge." Though the leaves seem at first glance to be wholly determined, they apparently have the choice between being destroyed and self-destruction. To the fascination of this possibility is added that of the esthetic qualities of the leaf on its final plunge. At this juncture the speaker, though aware of the problems of his world, still seems to have confidence in his outlook of individualism.

The next section, changed very little in revision, begins a comparison:

> You know who have waited by the wall
> The twilight certainty of an animal,
> Those midnight restitutions of the blood
> You know—the immitigable pines, the smoky frieze
> Of the sky, the sudden call: you know the rage,
> The cold pool left by the mounting flood,
> Of muted Zeno and Parmenides.

Apparently the speaker is addressing Tiresias, who waited by the wall of Thebes; and he feels that his own waiting here for illumination makes him in some respect identical with the ancient Greek. This modern man knows that the Greek's central problem is also his own: the problem of man. Tiresias is equipped to understand, and the speaker emphasizes the range of his experience.

He starts at the most primitive level—the animal. But the "restitutions of the blood" are precisely what modern man is incapable of achieving. As a further element in his catalogue, the pines are "immitigable" because he is projecting into them his own emotional need for permanence in nature. The "smoky frieze of the sky" likewise interprets nature in terms of the speaker's emotional need—this time to make it comprehensible within the framework of his inheritance of ideas from the Graeco-Roman world. The "cold pool left by the mounting flood" suggests a still higher need based on the problems of permanence and change. This idea is especially reinforced by the mention of Heraclitus (instead of Zeno) in the original version. Seemingly, the original speaker had in mind the conflict between the stress on becoming in Heraclitus and on being in Parmenides. The lack of agreement between those ancient philosophers finds its counterpart in the mind of twentieth-century man. Tate's change in the final version of the poem from Heraclitus to Zeno and the addition of the line "The cold pool left by the mounting flood" emphasizes the likeness of these ancient philosophers in skepticism. And in this quality they are especially modern.

Tiresias, knowing all, understands the close balance of life and death. In the earlier version of the poem he is said to praise the "immodest circumstance" of those who fall. But certainly "arrogant" in the later version conveys much more clearly the suggestion of the death wish in the speaker. His sense of futility was markedly emphasized in the shift from the line of the Fugitive anthology, "Here at this stile, once more, you know it all," to "Here by the sagging gate, stopped by the wall."

The section beginning "Turn your eyes to the immoderate past" represents momentary elation on the part of the speaker as he glimpses the possibilities of free choice given to the dead Confederates. The changes incorporated into the later versions of the section seem mostly intended to emphasize this element of free choice. The line "Find there the inscrutable infantry rising." The possibility of freedom of will seems much greater in the second, especially because of the repetition of "turn" from the preceding line. And earlier versions of the poem compared the infantry with "The demons out of the earth," an apparent reference to the demons of Gadarene, which Matthew, Mark, and Luke agree in calling inhabitants of the tombs. In the final version of the poem, the line became "Demons out of the earth." This change removes the deterministic implications of the Biblical story and shifts the speaker's emphasis to the freedom of choice of the avenging spirits.

When the speaker begins to call the famous Civil War names, he is attempting to find meaning in the concreteness of the individuals and events of that struggle. Because he resists the deterministic implications of mass movements or gatherings of men, he tries to find it in the qualities of men like Jackson and in deeds such as those of Albert Sidney Johnston at Shiloh. The earlier speaker concluded his meditation with, "In the orient of that economy/You have cursed the setting sun." Both "orient" and "economy" are used figuratively—the one for "east" and the other for "arrangement" or "dispensation." And the idea seems appropriate for Tiresias, whose foreknowledge must have caused him to regret the passing of such a race of emotionally integrated men. But the later version: "Lost in that orient of the thick-and-fast/You will curse the setting sun" allows the speaker to project his own ideas into the mind of Tiresias. Psychologically, it is much the more appropriate utterance. And poetically, the omission of "economy" is a great gain, for its connotations of the world of affairs remain with it even in another context.

The same kind of alteration is to be seen in the handling of the concept of silence in the "mummy" section. In the earlier version it was said to "engulf"; in the latter, to "smother." Because the speaker is given to personification as a means of understanding, the later version seems more appropriate. The mummy, which appears in both versions, suggests very well the personal element in the mind of the speaker. It also raises many problems: the decline of civilizations, the futility of man's effort to defeat the operation of time, the relationship of man and the hereafter. But the speaker in the earlier version is far more conscious of his figure: he makes it a simile and adds "whose niche/Lacks aperture." In later versions this idea is pruned away, and the figure stands alone, far more effective than when embellished. The deletion also allows for the close juxtaposition of mummy and hound bitch, also a later addition. Both express the tension between freedom and necessity which is uppermost in the speaker's mind. And both are reinforced by the religious tones of the "salt of their blood" section, which implies one solution in the speaker's mind for the problem of necessity.

Unsatisfied, the speaker turns his questions toward the individual. The speaker of the earlier version says: "What shall we say of the dirty sons/Whose legs and arms, guts, heads and teeth/ Stretched out the justice of efficiency?" And in the final version, these lines are replaced by:

> What shall we say of the bones, unclean,
> Whose verdurous anonymity will grow?
> The ragged arms, the ragged heads and eyes
> Lost in these acres of the insane green?

Both are questions about the problem of identity. The true essence of the men has been merged with something larger, as suggested by the mingling of the "salt of their blood" with the ocean. But there remains the question of the individual. His meaning must have to do not only with the "malignant purity" of his ideal essence, but with his uncleanness as well. The first speaker solves his problem by using a catalogue of anatomical detail. The effect intended is that of shock. But in the final version, Tate mitigates the starkness of this effect by allowing his speaker to merge the soldiers with the nature in which they rest. Nature and the memory of the men are transformed together. The personification is suitable to his solipsism, and his reverie does seem more philosophically satisfying than that of the first speaker. But this gain is bought at the risk of seeming slightly sentimental. For the speaker is obviously thinking of himself and his plight at also being lost in the "acres of the insane green."

The passage which follows, common to all versions of the poem, brings in spiders, owl, and willows. These conventional death symbols all have overtones of determinism. They imply the history of which the soldiers are a part; it is as important a part of their meaning as their future. Still another aspect of their meaning is suggested in the synesthesia of "invisible lyric."

The physical and the spiritual are mysteriously brought into relationship even in the song of the screech owl.

The next sections concern the consequences of the meditation in the graveyard. In the earlier version, the transition is made rather abruptly:

> We have not sung, we shall not ever sing
> In the improbable mist of nightfall
> Which flies on multiple wing;
> It has only a beginning and an end;
> And in between the ends of distraction
> Lurks mute speculation, the patient curse
> That stones the eyes, or like the jaguar leaps
> For the jaguar's image in a jungle pool, his victim.

This modern man realizes that he cannot achieve that creativity which will give meaning to the physical and spiritual sides of his nature. His is the problem of an overemphasis on a sterile rationality, which eventuates in skepticism. Because his philosophical outlook requires a projection of himself into what he perceives, his use of the insect figure is significant. It implies a parody of human consciousness and human creativity. Perhaps he can sing, but only with a voice which emphasizes, even more than the voice of the screech-owl, his sterility. The figure of the jaguar follows appropriately in his meditation because he is obviously post-Darwinian in thought. It implies the individualism that must result from his skepticism—an individualism that is ultimately self-destructive.

The final version of this section employs the same figures, somewhat rearranged:

> We shall say only the leaves whispering
> In the improbable mist of nightfall
> That flies on multiple wing;
> Night is the beginning and the end
> And in between the ends of distraction
> Waits mute speculation, the patient curse
> That stones the eyes, or like the jaguar leaps
> For his own image in a jungle pool, his victim.

For this speaker, the possibility of creativeness seems much more remote than for his predecessor. He can only contemplate. The voice of the leaves is reduced to a mere whisper; he implies that there is for him no individual choice, only the determinism of science. Because he can have only a limited possibility of significant action, his capacity for struggle is likewise limited. If this is true, then he must be a lesser man than his predecessor. He may even be a sentimentalist who uses his philosophy as an excuse to avoid the possibility of action.

But in the section of the poem which follows, he is partially saved, as was his predecessor, by "knowledge carried to the heart"—his direct apprehension of the world of symbols. Despite the poet's word to the contrary, the speaker seems anything but resigned to the idea that the grave is all. The answers to his questions about the grave seem clearly to be negative, especially in light of the adjective in "the ravenous grave."

The last section in the first version of the poem began: "Leave now/The turnstile and the decomposing wall." In the final version of the poem, this became: "Leave now/The shut gate and the decomposing wall." The finality of the observer's statement seems much stronger in the later version. The turnstile as a form of the wheel is an effective symbol of determinism. But it also implies mechanism, one feature of which is the idea of reversibility. The "shut gate" carries the idea of finality much more strongly. The Confederate cemetery thereby becomes a kind of Eden from which man is finally locked out. And the figure of the serpent, to which the speaker's mind now turns, seems natural in this context. It is linked not only with time, but also with knowledge and with evil. The fact that it is a "gentle serpent"— a silkworm—allows it to suggest the thread of life and the Fates as well as scientific determinism.

The last line of the early version of the poem was: "See him— what he knows—he knows it all!" In the final version, it becomes: "Sentinel of the grave who counts us all!" The first version makes explicit the symbolism of the serpent-silkworm; the later assumes it. Perhaps the most subtle feature of the final version is its use of the pronoun, which personifies the grave. By identifying himself with the grave, the speaker has comprehended it. His is a personification appropriate to a counting man of modern science. Yet the tone is matter of fact, and the speaker seems resigned.

Tate's achievement—and it goes without saying that he must be judged on the final version of his poem—is both philosophical and esthetic. The careful selection of the concrete materials of his poem enables him to suggest the vast complexity of problems which beset modern man. And his speaker's mind is such as to encompass a set of reactions to these problems and to suggest an adjustment to his age possible for twentieth-century man. In a sense this might be described as bravery. Caught up in the history, philosophy, and science of his age, he might easily have become self-pitying. But his figures show a high degree of control. Perhaps it is not too much to find him brave in a sense that few of Hemingway's characters ever are. For Tate required not only that the intellect be placed under control, but the emotions as well.

II "*Mother and Son*"

Tate's ability to compress psychological complexity into the smallest possible space is well illustrated in "Mother and Son."[5] Essentially, this poem is a little drama; it might well serve to illustrate Eliot's thesis of the dramatic element in all poetry. Related from the standpoint of a detached observer, this poem creates the illusion of objectivity necessary for drama. This observer keeps his distance; he describes not hysterically but reasonably. His judicious use of a Latinate vocabulary elevates and dignifies his tone. The even pace of the lines and the frequent rhyme contribute to the illusion of control: this is a desinterested account of what has been a highly emotional relationship.

The succession of liquid consonants in the first line establishes the slow pace with which time is moving in the chamber of death. Evidently this tempo seems slow by comparison with what has preceded it. The man, it seems, has been vigorous; though he is not dead, he wishes he were because he is accustomed to maintaining the tempo of whatever he undertakes. His inattentiveness which "hastens the dark" amounts to a death-wish.

The condition of the son is doubtless explained, at least in part, by the attitudes of the mother. Her "white hand" indicates the over-refinement of the pseudo-aristocracy. And her "erect head" implies that she is not bowed down by grief even in the face of the death of her son. Her stare is directed not at the man's face but at his body. In her "importunate womanhood" and in her "hand of death" it is possible to see the kind of woman about whom Rimbaud wrote. She has deprived man of his innocence; it is she against whom man must be pitted. Though she is a mother, her motives in being a "compositor of blood" are those caused by excessive development of the will.

The second stanza provides some of the exposition of the drama; it does so by focusing attention on the mother's memories of what has taken place on this bed. His lying on the bed on which he was conceived and born seems a desire to recapitulate the sin of the father. By taking his father's place, he identifies himself with his father. Evidently the mother has told him of the sins of the father in order, like a vampire, to possess his soul for herself. His choosing to die in the same place as the father represents a drawing away from the mother and a closer identification with the father. His reasons for doing so are in part his unconscious awareness of the symbolic rightness of his act. In his state of alienation, his awareness of a burden of inherited guilt, and his sickness of soul, he is very much a man of the twentieth century.

The figure of "impenetrable day" at the close of the second stanza signals the beginning of a harsher tone. The mystery of his birth seems insoluble, especially as the mother is described in the next line as "falcon." That she would be a bird of prey whose attention is directed toward her own offspring seems a contradiction to his ideas of motherhood. The transference to motherhood of the falcon's ritual performance of duty makes the son a mere helpless victim. Perhaps her will is stronger than his; if so, he may be merely a self-pitying determinist. On the other hand, he may be saved by his ability to show some resistance.

His capacity for struggle is expressed in the figure of the manacle in the third stanza. True, the mother by her priority in time and by her aggressiveness has been able to establish ascendancy. But she has generated in him a resistance that matches her forwardness. His passiveness is not feminine; instead it conceals a steely resistance. She may be a Hedda Gabler who has a perverted longing to control a human destiny by helping it to achieve a beautiful death. But he is not one to concede very much to her. The light which she radiates does not suggest to him, as it does to her, any transfiguration. Instead, he veers to its opposite: if this is light, he prefers darkness. If this is the meaning of life, he will seek death. If this is what is known, he will seek the unknowable.

The fourth stanza uses the figure of the cuttlefish to express the operation of the memory. These creatures suggest in their individual capacities the random quality in the memory, but their mass movements imply determinism. In this view the memory is free and at the same time determined. In the speaker's imagination these creatures are poised between the eye—symbolic of the intelligence or soul—and the lid, representing the power of refusal. This interpretation of the consciousness is like that stressed by Bergson in his analysis of the mind as a filter. The figure of the cuttlefish expresses the ability of the memory to obscure or to focus its content. It can "rise to the air" in the impulse toward idealization, or it can "plunge to the cold streams" by probing the depth of man's experience. Both of these impulses are present in the man's mind. His lack of capacity to resolve this conflict has led him to consider the romantic gesture of self-immolation.

As a gesture, this reaction is in character, for the man is dominated by his emotions. The woman, on the other hand, has a "dry fury," which evidently is of the intellect. They are, then, living examples of the split between intellect and sensibility characteristic of modern man. That such a condition cannot be permanent is suggested by the figure of the seed which is introduced in line thirty. Like a plant, the son has been cut down—is "prone in his autumn." But the "seed blown upon the returning wind" implies that he must find renewal—that the sensibility must reassert itself.

There follows a picture of such a change of condition. The narrator addresses the man as "child" and asks that he wait until the sun has altered its position. Now it is apparently illuminating the north wall, and this fact expresses the ascendancy of the coldly intellectual individual. But in the afternoon it will illuminate the south wall, a condition that implies the coming dominance of people like Stendhal's Italians—passionate and understanding.[6] The flowered wall suggests the fruitfulness that will prevail with that change of condition. Because the woman will be out of place in that setting, the sun will seem as swift and dangerous to her as a snake. Its illumination will strike the symbol of her hypocrisy—the crucifix upon her breast. And with this illumination will come death for her because her essence demands the divided and hypocritical mind.

In the final stanza, the flies perform much the same function as they do in Miss Dickinson's "I heard a fly buzz" or in Dostoevsky's *The Idiot*. They suggest death by the very sluggishness of their lives. Their ability to survive the young man re-emphasizes the question of values. Still more ironical are the spiders, weaving their nests in between the artificial symbols of fertility. The most permanent thing about the room is the wallpaper—the most artificial and inconsequential thing about it.

The totality of the picture of modern life presented in this poem is consistent with those Tate had made in other poems. Afflicted by sordidness and ugliness, beset by problems of identity and determinism, it finds its only possible redemption in the art so pitifully represented by the wallpaper. This technique, learned much earlier from Eliot, Laforgue, and Corbière, had been transformed in Tate's handling. His earlier poems, such as "Nuptials," had shown that he could select the externally impressive detail. But in poems such as "Mother and Son," he had learned to select the detail that could finally and fully symbolize the human condition.

III "Sonnets of the Blood"

"Sonnets of the Blood" is a sequence of nine English sonnets,[7] which probably owes a good deal to Donne's *Holy Sonnets*. Tate uses the form in such a way as to give a sense of completeness in each sonnet: each could stand by itself as well as with its fellows. Even the individual quatrains tend to be compressed into blocks which have individual unity, but which at the same time also seek completeness in others. In this way the form itself helps to present an essential problem of the sequence: the question of the place of the individual in the group.

The first sonnet marks the speaker as a modern intellectual, concerned not merely with the rational but with the emotional as well. As his first question shows, he is analytical in his outlook, but his attitude is tempered by his interest in the creative and unifying qualities of myth. His imagination has the sweep necessary to encompass fundamental questions and to integrate past, present, and future.

The question with which the first sonnet begins is so phrased as to suggest an integration of three different impulses in the mind of the speaker: "Flesh and blood" implies the Christian, "compounded" is derived from the scientific, and "life of time" is drawn from the philosophical-historical. But the speaker's difficulty in bringing all these elements to fusion is soon apparent in the lines: "This prowling of the cells, litigious love,/Wears the long claw of flesh-arguing crime." "Prowling" gives the spermatozoa impulses like those of the cat, but the appositive "litigious love" raises the pitch and complexity of the emphasis on individualism by setting it against a figure drawn from the law. The polarity thus expressed between the very primitive and the civilized expresses the range of the problem. It was one understood by the Darwinians. Even though the tone of the battle over evolution may have shifted, the modern has never been freed of all the implications of its interpretation of life. Among these is the need for individualism, sometimes it would seem even to the point of criminality.

In the second quatrain the speaker makes a sudden shift to more hopeful tones. Instead of the scientific view of man as determined by his environment, he turns his glance to the example of the first settlers in America "of our bone": that is, "of our kind." The speaker transfers his legal figure to them to emphasize the exertion of the will which they were able to make as they "sued the dust." They, too, were limited by deterministic elements, described in a legal figure as "Estopped forever by the last dusted stone."

Their example provides the transition to the picture of brotherhood that he next paints. If it is possible for men to act together constructively, it seems a pity that brothers can be united only in their perception of their common evil. But because such understanding is likely to produce sympathy for the other's failings, it is called "treason to the murderous hour." Cain did not show much understanding of his brother Abel. But, the speaker observes, this identity of brotherhood should be a goal for all mankind.

In the second sonnet the tone becomes less formal as the subject matter seems to shift to a more personal emphasis:

> Near to me as perfection in the blood
> And more mysterious far, is this, my brother:
> A light vaulted into your solitude.
> It studied burns lest you its rage should smother.

The achievement of perfection in the blood has to do with the emotional responses, in the ability to feel at one with others in the fundamental identity of the race. But upon this edifice of sensibility is built the intelligence, symbolized in the second sonnet by the figure of light. This other side of man—"vaulted into your solitude"—is his singularity, which paradoxically can come only of his emotional achievement of identity with another human being.

The figure of light enables the poet to avoid a confusion with the perversion of individualism of the nineteenth-century evolutionists. He avoids giving it a mechanical quality; instead he personifies it to suggest volition. Once realized, this soul "studied burns," and the shift from pure light to a figure incorporating both heat and light suggests that this soul does not merely incorporate rationality. Instead, it brings together the fullness of an integrated sensibility and intellect; its complexity is implied by its radiation of both light and heat.

That complexity is emphasized in the lines:

> It is a flame obscure to any eyes,
> Most like the fire that warms the deepest grave
> (The cold grave is the deepest of our lies)
> To which our blood is the indentured slave.

Perhaps man's inability to understand is simply a function of the weakness of his intellect. But the figure of the flame adds another possibility: this obtuseness may be akin to the reaction described by the Grand Inquisitor to man's "terrible freedom." Because man is emotionally weak, he does not wish to assume responsibility for freedom or for enlightenment. Even though spiritual oneness with all mankind is implied in the figure of the flame and of the blood, this is not an unmixed blessing. Only those who are capable of becoming strong and aware can hope to achieve its benefits.

By using the figure of the fire that warms the grave, the speaker asserts the spiritual meaning of death. He repudiates the idea of the coldness of the grave as merely positivistic in order to emphasize the spiritual unity of mankind past and present. His reference to the blood as the slave of the flame that warms the grave emphasizes how much man's life is dependent on his spiritual unity with the past.

The third sonnet concerns the emotional attitude of those involved in the conflicts expressed in the first two sonnets. The speaker calls for dignity because it represents poise: this degree of self-awareness requires both humility and control. The second quatrain explains the brother's survival from infancy as the operation of dignity: death, personified as a considerate gentleman, "would hardly let you go."

The speaker then looks more deeply into the problem of dignity. Especially does he assert that poise is needed in the approach to that part of destiny outside the control of the will. The brother's attitude should not be one of contempt, for this would signify pride. He should reject the tendency to personify fate, and he should regard the moment of death objectively— as an "hour of chance." Though the figure of the stage in the last two lines of the sonnet seems to make a shift in tone, it recalls the first part of the sonnet. The speaker is aware of a certain element of play in his whole attitude toward necessity and death. When the individual is able to assume the perspective of the shroud, he will have little difficulty in achieving the humility of dignity.

The tone of the fourth sonnet is signaled by the cliché with which it begins and by the word *fuss*, which concludes the first line. The seriousness of the meditation immediately preceding is juxtaposed with the conversational. The speaker is being ironical; he is only mocking when he proclaims that people are different from those in earlier times and that the need for order is not still present: "Who of our kin was pusillanimous,/A fine bull galloping into a storm?" The figure of the bull, so far from ridiculing the speaker's Confederate ancestors, is intended to express the ridiculousness of the idea that those Southerners were strong-willed but stupid, wilfully courting inevitable disaster. The question implies, at least in part, an answer to the problem of determinism raised in Sonnet III. No doubt their ancestors found themselves in circumstances not entirely under their control. But they did not act from the will alone.

The following quatrain brings up the delicate problem of the balance between humility and pride, especially in the military man. The speaker declares that Southerners' ancestors —like all men—needed pride in order to be men. Yet in going to war they did not wear the trappings of the soldier self-consciously, but casually. And because their boots and spurs "went a devil's ride," their owners would soon have learned humility if they had not already possessed that quality.

The final quatrain and the concluding couplet are occupied with a story about Jefferson which illustrates within the Southern context the ability of a man to exercise freedom of choice even against a strong line of tendency. Instead of framing his actions to accord with those of his neighbors, Jefferson chose to accept the concept of nature as interpreted by the philosophers of the Enlightenment. He was a "tall" man—a favorite metaphor with Tate for nobility. And he "meditated calmly"—the taking of time which would perhaps imply a decision made according to his own free will. Yet ironically his decision reveals how difficult is the assertion of the will even for a philosopher: the decision he made only permitted him to take a pattern already worked out by others. And it was taken out of a kind of rivalry: he freed his slaves to be more free than they. So his freedom to act was, if not illusory, strictly limited.

Sonnet V moves the question of determinism into the present. The elder brother seems incapable of exercising any freedom of choice. He has been sent to the West. The region is described as "cyclonic"—subject to conditions uncontrollable by man; and the brother does not return of his own choice but is brought back. The speaker intimates that the elder brother is simply following a tendency in the disposition of the whole family. His going to the West has been a response to the "shaking fury in the track/We know so well." His is no doubt a romantic impulse, though seemingly an exercise of free choice. But the speaker makes it a quality innate in their dispositions: "wound in these arteries." Here "wound" has a double sense: first, it is as if the tendency were a thread wound into the arteries as a determining quality; and second, it brings to mind the twisting movement of the blood—especially the pulsing arterial blood, with its resemblance to a river. With this figure the reader is also reminded of the difference in sameness of the river of Heraclitus.

The latter alternative seems stronger in the admonition to the brother, for it implies that he might "study how to seize mortality." In this figure the speaker is playing upon a double sense of the infinitive "to seize": "to comprehend" in the sense of emotional understanding, which the brother by his long absence would seem not to know; to put this understanding into significant action. In the speaker's view, mortality is an active agent with a capacity "to derange corpuscles" according to its own design.

The use of the synecdoche here enables the speaker to imply that the blood, despite its seeming shapelessness, actually has its own inner form. The fact that he believes that the blood has been altered by the death of the mother suggests that he had in mind an idea analogous to that advanced by T. S. Eliot in "Tradition and the Individual Talent"—that each succeeding art-work alters the entire corpus accumulated from the past.[8] So the blood as symbolic conveyor of the history of the race is altered by each succeeding individual. Especially in death is the alteration effected by the individual likely to be made clear.

In Sonnet VI the speaker employs a honeysuckle figure which emphasizes his consciousness of his own decadence. His awareness may seem to give him a certain effeteness, but he does not surrender entirely. "Not half so stout" is a homely Southern country idiom that gives the impression that he has a reserve that is anything but decadent.

Thinking of his mother's death, the speaker asserts: "So think upon it how the fire burns blue/Its hottest, when the flame is all but spent." Though he is conscious of being the heir of those who had spiritual intensity, this "Thank God the fuel is low" makes him seem as if he is using an argument from determinism to rationalize a failure to act. His cry "we'll not renew/That length of flame into our firmament" implies a failure of will rather than a failure of resources; and this idea corresponds closely with Tate's own view, often reiterated, of the spiritual condition of modern man. The figure of the flame reaching the firmament reveals the speaker's lingering faith in idealism. Perhaps it is just this residual belief that makes for his difficulty.

He believes, but only enough to understand—not enough to act.

In the final quatrain and couplet, he amplifies the force of this idea. He visualizes the mother as a priestess at whose altar the flame has burned so intensely that the temple itself has been set aflame. The rooftree which is about to fall is a punishment to those who had dared to look too closely at the sacred mysteries. The mother, whose symbolic qualities are emphasized in her appurtenances of the big chair, the black shawl, and the crucifix, is perhaps responsible: she is said to be "burning with motherly light/More spectral than November dusk could mix/ With sunset." The ambiguity of his expression, especially in the use of "spectral," emphasizes the difficulty of his basic problem: among the things which have determined him is the gift of "light," or intelligence, by which his will would seem to be free.

The thought of dissolution in Sonnet VI leads naturally to the contemplation of possible preparations for death in Sonnet VII:

> This message hastens lest we both go down
> Scattered, with no character, to death;
> Death is untutored, with an ignorant frown
> For precious identities of breath.

Character—uniqueness or individuality—seems to be the speaker's requirement for immortality. This ability to differentiate himself from others is opposed in his mind to the chaos of death. Yet this differentiation seems to depend upon finding a system of order: the term "identities" stands against "scattered" and "confusion." In his value-system a heavy premium is placed upon arrangement as a clue to worth, even though it does reduce his freedom of choice.

In his system, evil seems to be expressed in a personification of death, of which the main attribute is ignorance. His association of the chaos with evil and his choice of the vulture figure to express this condition help to identify him with Prometheus. If the speaker accepts the attribution of the Titan's ability to perceive to himself, he dissociates himself from his martyrdom. For he says that he has never actually seen the vulture; he has only "heard the echoes in a dark tangled wood." Though he has the ability to perceive, he does not have the character to act.

Man's terrible aloneness, caused by his emotional deficiency, has the result, the speaker says, that "We fulminate, in exile from

our earth,/Aged exclusions of blood memories—/Those supersti-
tions of explosive birth." These "aged exclusions" have to do
with the overemphasis on the intellect which is so much a feature
of the modern consciousness. The figure of the explosive expresses
the vehemence with which such an emphasis must be made to
deny the imperious demands of the emotions. And it also suggests
the desperation of the men who need to shut themselves off
from themselves in this manner. The superstition of the intellect
—and the speaker is clearly thinking of Bacon—was born of
man's Faustian pride. Because man cannot forever deny his
sensibility, Death must be the eventual end of his failure to
achieve self-knowledge.

Sonnet VIII begins with a reference to the faith of modern
man: the speaker mentions first the power which man actually
worships and second "the storied hand of God," to which man
pays lip service. The condition is such that the speaker describes
it in death symbols: the buzzard hovers over the scene, and
spiders which are "eating their loves" denote modern men. Even
though these creatures are associated with individualism and
determinism, their actions imply a perverted awareness of others
and a freedom of choice. The speaker's application to them of
"self-devouring shame" implies that man is conscious of responsibility—that he has exercised his free choice in arriving at
his present condition. The expression, too, is a reminder of the
death of Arachne in Ovid's story. Athena's restoration of the
suicide seems to offer some hope, even to the self-centered
modern.

But the myths of the house of Atreus offer smaller ground
for optimism:

> Call it the house of Atreus where we live—
> Which one of us the Greek perplexed with crime
> Questions the future: bring that lucid sieve
> To strain the appointed particles of time!

The figure of the sieve has a passive, mechanical quality,
expressive of the tendency of modern science to operate coldly
and unemotionally. It has enormous power to reject so as to
retain only the small particle apropos of its problem. The
speaker's use of the word "appointed" to describe the retained
particles makes implicit commentary on the controlling deter-

minism of scientific thought. But he concludes this meditation with at least a qualified assertion of freedom of choice. Man can choose, he says, between Corinth and Thebes—Corinth, the happy place to which Pegasus returned each night, and Thebes, the seat of the house of Atreus.

Beginning the ninth sonnet with "captains of industry," Carlyle's term for industrialists, the speaker rejects by his irony all the fatuous optimism of the nineteenth century. He indirectly rejects the doctrine of progress because of its failure to establish goals; from his vantage point, it is comparatively easy to see an aimlessness in the nineteenth century. The speaker, taking Carlyle's prophetic stance, warns that the actions of the captains of industry call up inevitable reactions—"harsh velleities of time."

More imperiously, he addresses his brother, "captaining your hour," with the admonition that his power is only temporary. He employs a figure from mathematics to emphasize the excessive stress on the rational in modern technology: "false division" will leave nothing of the essential life of the sensibility. Then the figures become more foreboding: he hints that our modern, refined Attic civilization may be overpowered by the rude Thracian barbarians whose emotional life is yet intact. Worse still, he uses a figure based on *The Golden Bough,* in which the old king is being sought by one who would kill him and be his successor.

The sonnet concludes with a figure of the sea as a symbol of eternity. Technological man with his petty engines thinks to keep out the sea from the land. But this holding back of infinity by mere mechanical contrivance cannot endure, and the man who tries it will be overwhelmed. For infinity cannot be comprehended by the devices of the finite mind, which are always more simple than reality itself.

What this poem attempts to do, then, is extraordinarily complex: it is no less than an analysis of the content of the modern sensibility. To analyze so much, Tate arranges a series of symbols into a pattern which allows them to reach out for their full range of extension and intension. He is thereby enabled to condense into little more than Poe's limit for the poem a content very much larger than "The Raven." This is an extraordinary intellectual feat, but he is not merely performing poetic gymnastics. His aim was what Poe's prescription implied that the poem should achieve: intensity of presentation. What a philosopher might have taken many pages to say, Tate has said in a few. And by sharpening the focus, he has actually said much more. The comparison in the final analysis is invalid, for what Tate has said could be stated in no other way. In the remarkable concreteness of his utterance his poetic accomplishment is most abundantly realized.

IV *Conclusion*

On the surface the 1937 volume of poetry appears little different from its predecessors. The old themes still remain Tate's subject matter: the split between sensibility and intellect, the philosophical opposition to positivism, the call for unity with the cultural tradition. The reiteration of these themes serves to emphasize their usefulness to the poet. Apparently he was convinced of their philosophic truth, but their real importance to him was their ability to give consistency to his poetry. No doubt he was aware of Eliot's belief that the poet need not be an original philosopher, and he was certainly not attempting to be one.

But his poetry was increasing in effectiveness and in originality. Paradoxically, these qualities derived from the reduction of the romantic element in his poetry. The objective presentation of a subjectivity had always been a basic element of Tate's technique, as it has been for so many modern authors. But this illusion is very difficult to control because every nuance of the speaker's figures, tone, and rhythm must form a part of an organic whole. Tate's earlier poems tended to draw attention to the subject himself. He usually seemed to insist on the importance of his own reactions. Inevitably he gave the impression of being fond of his own ability to perform for himself, and so he reduced his credibility as a witness.

In these 1937 poems, however, the speaker's tone is much more subdued. By placing much more material within the observer's line of vision, Tate reduces his speaker's self-consciousness and makes him far more objective. Not only is the fact of subjectivity objectified, but the material within the compass of that subjectivity is made more objective. By increasing the distance between his observer and the material observed, the eye is made to encompass more. In "To a Romanticist" the observer's eye focuses closely upon a single, emotionally complex figure. But the ability of the observer to fix his attention on important matter seems much greater in the "Ode to the Confederate Dead." For there, history, philosophy, and science are all brought together and focused within one pattern. The gain in objectivity for the finished poem is immense. Because this quality is apparent in most of Tate's work at this period, it is entirely fair to assert that he is much the more an artist for the achievements of this volume.

CHAPTER 7

The Fathers

BY THE 1930's the American public had read such a long succession of Southern novels that the type had become firmly established. Not everyone, of course, recognized that the formula had become a rigid fixity; on the surface there seemed to be great differences between individual books. Wolfe's *Look Homeward, Angel* did not much resemble Mitchell's *Gone With the Wind,* and Caldwell's *God's Little Acre* certainly did not seem to have much in common with Young's *So Red the Rose.* Yet all of these novelists were using Southern settings romantically. For each of them, as for many of their predecessors, the South was a region in which ordinary human limitations did not apply. Extremes of heroism or of degradation not only were possible in that enchanted land, but they were the very qualities expected by the public.

It is little wonder, then, that some of the reviewers were puzzled by Tate's *The Fathers* when it appeared in 1938. The *Saturday Review* averred that people would not understand Tate's indirection and inconclusiveness. Observing that the work of the novelist ought to be the creation of knowable human beings in understandable relationships with each other, this reviewer declared that in his opinion Tate had not succeeded.[1] In the *Nation* another baffled reviewer tried to read *The Fathers* as a conventional historical novel. Unfavorably comparing George Posey of *The Fathers* with Rhett Butler of *Gone With the Wind,* the writer found that Tate's character lacked the qualities to make him three-dimensional. Because this reviewer felt that a historical novel ought to stress action, she declared that Tate ought to have known better than to use a bloodless old bachelor to narrate his story.[2]

Fortunately, other reviewers did not so completely miss the mark. Henry Steele Commager stressed the psychological elements in the story,[3] and John Peale Bishop emphasized Tate's conception of the social order.[4] But taken as a whole, the early reviewers did remarkably little to illuminate the work. Not until 1947 was a substantial critical study of *The Fathers* published—that of Arthur Mizener in *Accent*. His essay, illuminating enough to be republished several times, remains the best study of Tate's novel. But it is difficult to see why a book, called by Mizener "one of the most remarkable novels of our time,"[5] should not have attracted more scholarly and critical interest.

I *Lacy Buchan: The Making of a Modern Sensibility*

The Fathers is narrated entirely by Lacy Buchan, who is telling the story in 1910 when he is sixty-five years old and retired from the practice of medicine. His motives for telling the story seem threefold. First, because he feels guilt about his part in the final horrors of the action, he may be trying to atone for his sin by confession. Second, he is trying to recapture the emotional qualities of the formative period of his life. And, third, he is attempting to grasp the full intellectual meaning of the part of his experience relevant to his present condition. The pressure of his curiosity about himself and his associates gives the book its momentum and interest.

In choosing the first-person point of view, Tate ignored Henry James's admonition in the Preface to *The Ambassadors*. James had warned that a novel recounted entirely in the first person is "foredoomed to looseness."[6] James's observation, it would seem, had something in common with that of Aristotle in the *Poetics:* the unity of the hero is not enough to unify the drama.[7] The temptation, James thought, was for the novelist to use the mind of the first-person narrator as a convenience to avoid creating the full illusion of unity. Tate could have seen in a book like *Huckleberry Finn* the wisdom of James's advice. The consciousness of Huck gives the book interest and apparent unity. But the contradictory attitudes inevitably present in the created illusion of a complex human being help to make the unity of the novel at least doubtful.

The point of view of *The Fathers* is very different from that of *Huckleberry Finn*; it is much more like that of the opening section of *Swann's Way*. Like Proust's narrator, Lacy Buchan is trying to reach across the gap of memory to recover what was emotionally significant in his youth. Little of that experience is recoverable. What does return comes with a certain remoteness, but this is an advantage: it enables Tate to give "distance" to what is subjective in the life of the younger Lacy. Because of this "distance," what was once subjective becomes objective: the elder Lacy looks at the younger with interest but also with some detachment. His mind provides a standard by which all the experience in the novel can be judged. When Lacy writes about his father, for example, the reader does not see the older man entirely through the emotions of an adolescent; he also has available the judgment of the elder Lacy. The presence of this quality throughout the book tends to give it logical and emotional unity.

It is quite otherwise with a book like *Huckleberry Finn*, in which Mark Twain relied on the unfolding of a mind in action—upon an almost pure subjectivity. Much of the charm of that book depends upon the illusion of frankness with which the boy tells about his experiences. The reader goes willingly enough from incident to incident; but, without the standard of judgment provided by a Proust or a Tate, the reader finds it very difficult to reconcile the Huck on the Phelps plantation with the Huck of the river.

There is no such problem with the characters of *The Fathers*. Though the individuals are no more consistent with themselves than any others, their development becomes a matter for objective contemplation in the mind of the elder Lacy Buchan. Even the subjectivity of the young Lacy is brought under the control of this point of view. This first-person narrator is a device that Mark Twain and James seemingly did not envisage. He is the strongest element in the novel for giving a tight, logical organization to what would otherwise have been merely a loose accumulation of incident.

The novel also opens on a Proustian note: the narrator experiences involuntary recall set in motion by a sensation that repeats a previously experienced sensation. In Proust's novel, the taste of a madeleine soaked in tea triggers Marcel's recall of his Aunt Léonie.[8] In the same manner, Lacy Buchan's getting a whiff of salt fish causes him involuntarily to recall the roe herring which his Aunt Myra was serving at his mother's funeral. Associated with this sensation are others: the taste of the salt in the fish, the sound of Uncle Armistead's "Hanh?," the black of the coffin, and the white of the room.[9] Though the combination of these sensations is quite arbitrary, they have become fixed together in a pattern of emotional meaning for Lacy. In this respect they fulfill—at least for Lacy—T. S. Eliot's formula for the objective correlative.[10] On the surface the sensations which form the objective correlative of this emotional experience seem trivial; actually Tate chooses those which have important symbolic content.

The fish served at the funeral obviously has to do with the early symbol for Christ. By extension, it is also a symbol of baptism. While reminding those at the funeral of these Christian ideas, the fish doubtless also suggested to them a last communion, one ironically to be fulfilled better than they knew. Because the Buchan family had a considerable amount of Classical learning, the participants may also have been aware of the custom in the cult of Adonis of using the fish as an offering to the dead. This food at the funeral meal, then, is a reminder of the family's participation in its cultural heritage, both the Christian and the Classical.

The sound which Lacy remembers best from his mother's funeral is the pathetically ludicrous "Hanh?" of Uncle Armistead. Because age had so reduced the old man, this sound was practically his only speech. And in some sense it represented the man himself. Because Uncle Armistead in the feebleness of his life illustrates the mortality of all men, his sound comes to stand for the human condition itself. Uncle Armistead's "Hanh?" as speech has a much larger content than appears on the surface. He was requesting enlightenment; he knew that he was not always a vegetable. He was registering a desire for communion with others; his enforced isolation oppressed him as much as it might have when he could communicate better. Ironically, then, he reminded those present of the intellectual and emotional constituents of their humanity.

Uncle Armistead's extreme age made Lacy aware of the past that the old man symbolizes. Born at the end of the Revolution, perhaps he might have taken advantage of the time to achieve greatness. But Uncle Armistead was not great. As Lacy examined him sleeping at the funeral, he found what seemed to him a clue. On the side of his thin, hooked nose Lacy discovered a tuft of gray bristles—to him "an evil looking mark." And Lacy remembered that at the age of ten Uncle Armistead had cursed God. Retribution followed when his wife died at twenty-six. And Lacy obviously felt that Uncle Armistead was still under a curse. Like Swift's Struldbrugs he was aware of all the satisfactions of the human state, but they could only tantalize him. Not for him was the greatness of a Jefferson; he could only be tolerated at the funeral and put in the care of the little Negro boy. The picture that Uncle Armistead made is not unlike that of Eliot's "Gerontion," and the emotions that he felt are doubtless no happier than those expressed in that poem.

Among the symbols which Lacy associates with the day of the funeral, some appeal to the sense of sight. Tate explained in "The Symbolic Imagination: the Mirrors of Dante" that sight must be pre-eminent for the poet.[11] Perhaps just for this reason, the black coffin seems more conventional than the other symbols associated with the day of the funeral. It is true that the blackness of the coffin symbolizes grief, and its placement in a long white room tends to emphasize the starkness of the grief. The white, indicative of a terrible lifelessness, overwhelms the point of blackness in the room. The mother is lost in a pattern of absolute colors and geometric design. This emphasis on the finality of the loss seems especially appropriate as it is remembered by the elder Lacy, for he can now see that actually as well as symbolically his mother's death marked the end of the old order.

While stressing the artist's need to emphasize sight, Tate also points out that men, like other animals, live by touch.[12] This sensation is best illustrated by Lacy's use of the piece of leather strap which he kept in his pocket. He acquired it on the day of the tournament in 1858 by picking it up in the yard when Uncle Coriolanus was not looking. His concealment of his theft from the old Negro probably had nothing to do with any punishment that might have been administered. Perhaps he was merely trying to outwit that guardian of the world of horses and men.

By stealing a fetish associated with the purely masculine world, he was in effect proving his manhood. And as he continued to carry the strap, it became the symbolic reminder of his youth. On the day of his mother's funeral, two years after he had found the strap, he was still carrying it in his pocket. Touching it was the formula for bringing back the day of the tournament, with its several symbolic indications of his change from youth to manhood. Particularly significant was its reminder of George's attempt to precipitate the boy into manhood with the present of a gun. No doubt his failure to fire the gun successfully left him with a certain yearning for manhood, of which the strap served as a reminder.

This yearning was intensified on the day of his mother's funeral by his attempts to make love to Jane Posey. His attempts, quite naturally, were frustrated by his elders. And probably because they were, she became the unattainable goal which grew more attractive the more it was pursued. A year afterward, when the Civil War had already begun, he was staying in Georgetown with his sister's family. Jane was likewise living there, and it seemed for a time that his pursuit might be successful. But again he was frustrated, this time harshly and rudely by the competition of his brother Semmes and by the intervention of Yellow Jim. Lacy's physical pursuit of Jane necessarily ended when she entered a convent. But she was transformed into an ideal, which Lacy has apparently kept for the remainder of his life.

All this time he carried the piece of strap with him. But when he was finally ready to join the Confederate Army, one of his last acts before going was to visit his old room at Pleasant Hill. And there he was reminded of the old piece of strap, now discarded behind the door. Because he had become a man, he could afford to dispense with this symbol which had so frequently given coherence to his experience.

Because Lacy has lived so largely by his memory, it is natural that he seek to understand its function. At one point in his narrative, he breaks into analysis: "Memory is all chance, and I have learned that you remember things not because they are important; you remember the important things because they help you to fix in mind the trifles of your early life, or the trifles simply drag along with them through many years the incidents that have altered your fortunes."[13] Much later he says that "you remember what you cannot understand."[14] He is evidently trying to interpret the memory according to the patterns of the reason; as a result, he makes it seem arbitrary. But this is only the intellectual side of Lacy speaking. In his concrete experience there is a much fuller presentation of Lacy's processes of memory. Just as it was right for Marcel to remember the madeleine soaked in tea, so it was right for Lacy to remember the smell of the salt fish. Memory is clearly a part of Lacy's uniqueness; its operation offers him at least some individuality in his twentieth-century world.

Another function of Lacy's memory which serves to establish the value of his point of view is the fact that his memory omits so much. This depiction of the mind in the act of focusing becomes of special usefulness in an artistic presentation. By its use, all the distractions and irrelevancies are removed from the interpretation that Tate wishes to present. He does not, for example, seem particularly receptive to the doctrine of progress. A major function of Lacy in the novel is his ability tacitly to interpret by his omissions as well as by his ability to remember.

His basic purpose in the novel is to give a controlling center of interpretation according to a twentieth-century sensibility. This is interpreted as an outlook extremely sensitive to symbolism, aware of history and interested in causation, and more than a little skeptical and pessimistic.

II *Major Buchan: A Neo-Classical Sensibility*

The Major Lewis Buchan who appears to the reader of *The Fathers* is the result of a double refraction: he is first of all the father seen through the eyes of an adolescent. Although the young Lacy seems mature for his years, his failure to notice his father's shortcomings hints at youthful idealization. He resents his brother Semmes's mentioning his father's inability to make more than fifteen bushels of corn an acre. He does not object to the father's carelessness in leaving his estate poorly planned for those who will inherit it. And he does stress the father's good qualities of scholarliness, kindness, and firmness. Lacy does not seem compulsive about this idealization, but he is consistent.

The second refraction for which the reader must allow is that of the elder Lacy Buchan. Most of the past for him is gone irrevocably; he says,

there is not an old man living who can recover the emotions of the past; he can only bring back the objects around which, secretly, the emotions have ordered themselves in memory, and that memory is not what happened in the year 1860 but is rather a few symbols, a voice, a tree, a gun shining on the wall—symbols that will preserve only as much of the old life as they may, in their own mysterious history, consent to bear.[15]

This process of symbolic reduction means that a great deal has been omitted from the father's portrait. As Martin Foss points out in *Symbol and Metaphor in Human Experience*, the symbol always requires that the part stand for the whole.[16] If the symbol stands for a great deal, it also omits a great deal. The result is that the portrait of the father is stylized—frozen in certain attitudes by the symbol-seeking mind of the old man Lacy Buchan.

Major Buchan symbolizes the Old South. The theory by which Lacy is enabled to imply so much about the essentially domestic activities of Major Buchan is contained in Lacy's belief that "as in all highly developed societies the line marking off the domestic from the public was indistinct."[17] Thus the private life of Major Buchan as depicted in the novel is quite sufficient to suggest the tone of the larger life of the public.

If Tate were a sociologist, he might have spoken of the South before the Civil War as a region of "culture lag." But for him the pejorative tone of such a classification would have been entirely wrong. Lacy Buchan makes a favorable interpretation of his father, whose spiritual connections were with the Neo-Classicism of the early days of the Republic. His agrarianism followed the ideas of Jefferson; as a way of life, it emphasized cultural as opposed to pecuniary values. It was self-sufficient and looked very little toward the urban culture of Europe. In continuing this pattern, the Buchans went to Alexandria only once a year and to White Sulphur Springs much more rarely. Their attachment to rural America was quite as strong as that of Thomas Jefferson.

It is no accident that Major Buchan had mannerisms that

have more to do with the eighteenth century than with the nineteenth. He iterated "Sir" in the manner of a Dr. Johnson. He used snuff, especially in times of stress, as his predecessors might have done. Toward the end of his life he even appeared in the knee breeches that had gone out of fashion years before. He read Gibbon, and he thought a portrait in Johnson's "The Vanity of Human Wishes" the most moving in English.[18] His formality of manner was derived from the sense of decorum of the Neo-Classic. If these smaller actions indicated the habitual, no doubt they represented more accurately Major Buchan's emotional inclinations than some of his larger choices. The limitations of the time might control his actions in an election, for example, so that he would appear a nineteenth-century man. But when he made personal choices, he was clearly disposed toward the eighteenth century.

Major Buchan also had a Jeffersonian attitude toward slavery. Though he seemed not to have violent scruples against the use of the slaves he had inherited, he had nothing to do with buying and selling them. When he disposed of slaves, he gave them their liberty and sent them to Pennsylvania. His relationship with Uncle Coriolanus grew more mellow as they grew older and the times more difficult. Their closeness was suggested in the scene in which Major Buchan told Coriolanus to sit down in the parlor and rest from his labors of house-cleaning. In this way, Lacy reported, the two old friends enjoyed each other's company.[19] It might seem that Lacy was here sentimentalizing the relationship between master and slave. But Uncle Coriolanus all along had had unusual status. He was, for example, concerned at the tournament about being in charge of the party. Evidently he had presided enough on such occasions to expect that dignity again. Time and again he acted as a substitute parent for Lacy, and the dignity of his bearing made him seem a much more likely surrogate parent than Jim of *Huckleberry Finn*, more likely also than Dilsey of *The Sound and the Fury*. And Lacy is not blind to the shortcomings of the slave system. He records the evil done to the Jack Lewis family, and he makes the treatment of Yellow Jim one of the recurrent themes of the story. His awareness of the evils of the system helps to give the impression that he is reporting accurately the picture of Uncle Coriolanus and Major Buchan.

A personal trait of the Buchan family which Lacy uses to show their emotional closeness to the eighteenth century is their lack of imagination. More than in any other member of the family, Lacy finds this quality in his father. When George Posey was trying to win Susan's hand, her father was acutely uncomfortable because he could not imagine that anyone would so flout the rules of decorum. George was able to win Susan partly because the Major did not have imagination enough to put himself in the place of an upstart like George.[20] The Major's Neo-Classical conventionality led him into more serious mistakes. When he turned the Jack Lewis family over to George to be released from slavery, he did not conceive that someone else might act on a different set of principles from his own. And his misjudgment of the magnitude of the secession movement came from his inability to visualize a territory outside his own. Beyond the Northern Neck of Virginia his imagination did not go.

Lacy implies that this lack of imagination is not entirely a weakness. It is true that the Major made certain errors, but they redounded less to his discredit than to that of others. This lack of imagination permitted the Major to accept convention, or an agreed-upon set of limitations on the individual man. He had by habit been accustomed to living within these prescribed limits, and he did not envisage even the possibility of going outside them. But Lacy—and in this judgment he is akin to Tate and Eliot and Hulme—feels that this is as it must be. Man is not infinite in possibilities as the Romantics thought him, but strictly limited. Because it is inconceivable that man can go beyond the limitations of his nature, he who understands these limitations can achieve the purposes of his life much better than the person who acts as if his possibilities are unlimited.

As Hulme had implied, the opening up of the infinite works both for good and for evil.[21] In Tate's novel the Civil War gives him the opportunity to demonstrate this principle. Because of his experience of the Civil War, Lacy understands how perilously near man always is to evil. By recognizing and approximating the need of man for limitations, the society of the Old South had enabled man to avert the worst of his evil possibilities. But exceeding these limitations opened up infinite possibilities for evil—a condition symbolized in *The Fathers* by the abyss. Because Lacy stresses so much the perils of living over the abyss, his acceptance of his father's conventionality seems plausible.

The interpretation of the Old South that Lacy offers through his portrait of his father differs markedly from those of many others who have interpreted the section. Mark Twain's notion that the ills of the South could be attributed to its reading of Sir Walter Scott is not far from the ideas of many scholars that the South was a hotbed of Romanticism. Romantic nationalism, racism, and individualism all have been among the formulas applied to the section. Despite the plausibility of some of the evidence for these interpretations, Lacy's stress on the Neo-Classical element in the Old South has merit. True, Lacy does admit the existence of certain newer romantic elements in Southern society—Sir Walter Scott is in the Buchan library, and the young men do joust in tournaments. But in his belief that the tone of Southern society was set by men like Major Buchan, he may have been right; for that society has always seemed conventional, restrained, and slow to change.

III   *George Posey: Romantic*

The picture of George Posey that first emerged in the mind of Lacy Buchan was a natural idealization. He was the man Lacy would have liked someday to be—young, handsome, and capable. He was a Lochinvar who stole Susan from the very grasp of her family. He could handle himself well in a tournament; he could fight a duel with honor and yet without killing anyone; and he could make money. All of these accomplishments marked him as a man to emulate.

What was more, he understood Lacy's emotional need for manhood, and he was prepared to give it in the form of a new gun. This symbolic present made such an impression on Lacy that he could never forget it. All through his narrative, Lacy stressed his attachment to George, even when his failings were most apparent. Now that Lacy has become an old man, he still cherishes his memory of George. And he does so despite his knowledge that George murdered his brother and caused his sister to lose her mind.

George Posey's face gave the essential clue to his character. His mouth was always smiling, but his eyes were cold. His mouth expressed the side of the personality he wished to turn to the world; it was under the control of the intellect. But the coldness of his eyes came from the soul; his sensibility was no match for his intellect. And he was under perpetual tension because of these two warring elements in himself.

The result of this dissociation in George is the outlook described by Eliot's "B" in "A Dialogue on Dramatic Poetry" when he said, "we know too much, and are convinced of too little."[22] In George, this want of conviction led him to become absolutely and destructively individualistic. His feelings, cut off from their normal channels in the personality, all became directed toward the personal. He was quite capable of feeling—perhaps even more intensely than most men—but he habitually denied his convictions. They fed on themselves, and in so doing became destructive of the man himself.

The split sensibility was the reason for George's breach of etiquette at the funeral of Lacy's mother. On that occasion he was essentially alone with his "locked-in" sensibility. He understood as well as anyone else the symbolic nature of the occasion and no doubt understood the pathos of the mother's death. But, unlike the Buchans, he did not have the perspective which would enable him to feel as well as to think that death is a part of life. His reaction then became a sentimental one—the identification of himself with the dead person. His excessive emotional reaction could find no acceptable outlet at the funeral, and he could think of nothing but escape. Ironically, this was even less acceptable to the Buchans, their servants, and associates than any other reaction would have been. They were accustomed to a society in which the individual found himself through a sensibility shared with others. Because George could only act individually, he became all the more conspicuous to those habituated to action within a framework of shared values.

In everything that George did, he was alone. Symbolically, his riding in the tournament probably showed him at his best. What was demanded in the joust was knowledge of power, and George was an expert with horse and lance. And his opponent, John Langton, was almost his match. He was another whose vacant eyes betrayed that he, too, was a victim of the split between sensibility and intellect. The altercation and duel between them that followed the tournament was the twin of their accomplishment. Because their emotions were all individual and personal, neither could regard the decision of the judges as anything but personal. Because George had won, he could easily conceal his personal interest. But John Langton displayed the same kind of bad manners that George had shown in asking the Major so abruptly for Susan for his wife. Essentially, both horsemen were interested in display of personal power, and neither was capable of controlling his emotions where personal prestige was involved.

The behavior of the combatants at the tournament provided a clue to the understanding of another event which was much more important for the fortunes of the main personages in the novel. On the day of the joust, Lacy saw the Negro, Yellow Jim, whom George Posey had exchanged for the horse he was riding in the tournament. From George's point of view, he had simply made an advantageous exchange of property. But he appeared not quite to believe in his own reasons, for he justified the exchange to Jim himself in words that Jim was to remember: "'Yaller Jim, you ain't done nothin'. You're liquid capital. I got to have money.'"[23] The cruelty of this speech would seem to have been unconscious; George was so accustomed to feeling only for himself that he had no appreciation of how his words would strike another.

Yet the humiliation of exchanging a man for a horse must have eventually come home even to a person accustomed to thinking only of himself. And certainly the sale of a house servant in the ante-bellum South must have been a step not to be taken lightly. Worst of all was the fact that Yellow Jim was George's half brother. Though Jim seemed to be in no position even to notice the relationship, unconsciously the set of his head betrayed a pride like that of all the Posey family. And he was obviously uncommonly intelligent. George in the blindness of his individualism was incapable of understanding that retribution might come even through the seemingly helpless Negro. Like many strong men, he underestimated the power of the weak.

Years later, after the Civil War had begun, Yellow Jim escaped and returned home to Georgetown. Because of the war he could not readily be sent back, and he was allowed to resume his old place. Aunt Jane Anne, his old mistress, treated him as if he had never been away. But the quiet tone of his reception belied the tensions which it engendered.

Even though George Posey was not physically present in his house during the enactment of its final tragedy, his spiritual presence had everything to do with what happened there. His wife Susan, Buchan that she was, did not approve of his wartime smuggling activities. She realized, no doubt, how much his "locked-in" ego was responsible for what he did. Instead of his gross individualism, she expected family loyalty and loyalty to some cause. But George was merely loyal to himself.

The resentment that George generated in Susan caused her to transfer to the whole Posey family the feeling she had about George. Particularly did she see in Jane another trap for the Buchans. She did her best to prevent her from seeing Semmes, and she encouraged Lacy to see her because she felt he was too young for a serious love affair. But she produced by reaction the very result she had been seeking to prevent. Semmes became ardent enough to ask Jane to marry him; and Lacy, as was only natural at his age, was but feeble competition.

All this time, Yellow Jim, the victim of George Posey's greed, had been in the house. Of all Yellow Jim's humiliations, none seemed more grievous to him than that his young mistress Jane no longer cared to have him near. It is not too much to see in this a sexual rejection. It was based, as Lacy says, on the Southern woman's natural fear of Negro men. But perhaps it might also have been based on his attractiveness to her; he was, after all, like her in being a Posey. By raping Jane, he simultaneously reunited himself with his own family and attempted its destruction.

Lacy interpreted this occasion as "the night that followed the brilliant day in May when the gay party rode away from Pleasant Hill for the gentleman's tilt."[24] Symbolically, the tournament had been the polite, stylized way of seeking for power. It was the brilliant surface for a set of values that had a much darker side. This new South represented here, by contrast with the older South of Major Buchan, was romantic. It fostered the men of split sensibility like George Posey and John Langton. These men were efficient, but they were also ruthless. Helpless people, like Yellow Jim and even Jane, were to them simply conveniences for their own use. Human beings for them were no different from machines to be used or coin to be counted.

The tragedy of Jane and Yellow Jim proved that such a set of values could only lead to ultimate disaster.

It is important for the symbolism of the tragedy that it took place in Georgetown, within Union territory. For if the new South was beginning to be infected with modernism, the North was the source of infection. Temperamentally, George Posey was completely at one with the spirit of the North. He was one of those of split sensibility and ruthless efficiency who would later make the world of the twentieth century in America. They would completely overwhelm those who had, according to Lacy, found a set of values that made life worth living. The relative inefficiency of this latter group made them no match for men like George, and the result of the encounter of the two could only be tragic.

George's war service for the Confederacy involved him in the first cause outside himself to which he had ever been dedicated. He admitted that he would have preferred to go with the North, with which he was temperamentally compatible. But he was persuaded by Semmes to go with the Confederacy, and the circumstances of his connections with the Alexandria Guards made it almost necessary that he continue his alignment with the South.

At first his participation was what might have been expected of a man of his inclinations. He was a smuggler, a man very necessary to the Confederacy because of its lack of industry. But for him it was mere opportunism, the chance to make a good trade. The occupation was full of danger, but this served merely to make it zestful. It was something to be done with the calculating intellect alone; his sensibility was not deeply involved.

The events which led to the murder of Yellow Jim and Semmes represented a culmination of the destructive element in the personality of George. After the rape of Jane, Susan pressed for Lacy to take Yellow Jim up the river. But Lacy had not yet achieved manhood enough to accomplish such a deed, and he thought mostly of letting Yellow Jim escape. But he hesitated, and in hesitating allowed time enough for Semmes to arrive. Susan knew the impetuosity of her brother and the lack of conviction of her husband. She tried with a threat to get George to do the deed himself, and he gave the appearance of complying. But he allowed Semmes to come with a loaded weapon. Semmes, true to his nature, shot Yellow Jim in an act of personal revenge. George, who retaliated instantly, killed Semmes and observed, "I never had any idea of killing that nigger."[25]

With this speech George expressed his experience of a reversal. For the first time he had really intended to do a generous act: setting Yellow Jim free would have constituted an acknowledgment of his own misdeeds toward the man. Probably an acknowledgment of brotherhood would have had to remain tacit, for this would have been more than his time and place would have found acceptable. But he would have had to forgive a crime against their own sister. This George was prepared to do, but he could not quite divorce himself from circumstance in the persons of Semmes and Lacy. And this was his undoing.

The Buchan family was finally able to forgive George because he was genuinely contrite. Despite his crimes against the family, he had become one of them. His experience taught him the need for integrating his intellect and his sensibility. He first discarded the role of smuggler. Then, in an act which indicated his humility, he appeared in the uniform of a Confederate private. He went through considerable danger to warn the family of an impending attack, and he drove away some Federal encroachers single-handedly. He did what he could to make reparation to Susan, for she was by then incurably mad.

But George could not change his character so easily, for his new-found humility was misinterpreted in the Confederate ranks. Insulted by John Langton, he could only reply by killing him. Service in the Confederate Army now being impossible, he could only change back to his disguise and escape to the Northern city of Georgetown. But he had shown young Lacy that it was possible for one such as he to act from the right motives after all. And this demonstration was enough to inspire Lacy's admiration and to continue to inspire it after the passage of nearly fifty years.

IV *Final Estimate*

The symmetry of form achieved in *The Fathers* reminds the reader more of Classical drama than of the meanderings of the stream-of-consciousness novel. George Posey goes offstage in the manner of an Oedipus, and Tate's emphasis seems almost to make this gesture a summary of the meaning of his life. The novel seems finally to point to something very nearly like this: the man who is victim of the dissociation of sensibility and intellect can be saved. By an act of the will, he can reintegrate his personality and take action based on the highest motives. Ironically, George's action seemed futile, but this only made his symbolic qualities more poignantly evident to Lacy.

Unfortunately for this thesis, the dissociation of sensibility and intellect seems too deeply rooted in George's fiber to be easily overcome. His earlier coldness removes him so far from genuine selflessness that the reader finds it difficult to believe that he could ever show genuine affection for another person. Whatever he may be supposed to have felt for Lacy comes through such a distance in the novel as to make him seem a projection of Lacy's youthful wishes and later remembrance. Instead of the fully rounded tragic hero, George gives the impression of the Byronic. George's last gestures did produce an effect, and it is difficult not to feel that he made them solely for that effect.

Tate's novel, then, illustrates again the difficulty for the artistic illusion which attempts to encompass a strongly deterministic thesis. Unless the human being can be given exercise of freedom, he tends to become a mere automaton. George Posey, never fully aware of his split sensibility, would seem never to have made a fully conscious struggle against it. And without struggle, the likelihood of his change seems remote.

Yet if the novel does not reach the first rank, it is an interesting achievement. Its handling of the memory theme might well have been the model for a school of imitators. But it seems to have attracted little notice, despite a reasonably good sale. And Tate did not follow up his achievement. Why, it is difficult to say. *The Fathers* remains, then, an isolated phenomenon in American letters, one that is only with difficulty coming into its rightful place.

CHAPTER 8

Tate the Critic

T HE SHARPLY POLEMICAL TONE of the title of Tate's first critical book was entirely in character for him. Ever since his Fugitive days, he had been known as a hard-hitting critic, one who based his criticisms on closely reasoned philosophical grounds. During his period in New York and later, he developed and extended this approach. Yet for some reason he did not gather his critical essays into a volume until 1936. After his Agrarianism had passed its peak, he issued his *Reactionary Essays on Poetry and Ideas*.

At the time he wrote, the literary world was sadly in need of a critic who would keep the attention of writers focused on fundamentals. The Depression had captured the interest of literary men as well as others, and various philosophies of overt action had gained currency. A poem or a novel perhaps would have seemed irrelevant to a starving man, and literary people, no more than others, wanted to be irrelevant. So literary men set out to reform the world. There was probably nothing wrong with their attempt to reform so long as it remained ancillary to their main purpose. But the reforming impulse tended to take over the writer entirely. And it tended to make him too much a determinist for literature. Almost always, he had to search for the causes of the evil he was seeking to reform. The literature of the 1930's all too frequently became mere propaganda.

The sharpness of tone in Tate's title signalled his opposition to this state of affairs. As is evident in all his work, he knew the pressure of determinism on the twentieth-century writer. He knew that the problem for the artist with regard to these issues is how to encompass the determinisms required by his age and yet to preserve something for freedom of choice. For without some freedom of the will, literature as such could hardly exist.

Tate's method of meeting this problem was to insist on the literary quality of literature. He directed his efforts, as he said in his preface to *Reactionary Essays,* against those who were "trying to make an art respectable by showing that after all it is only a branch of politics."[1] There are several ironies in Tate's expression, not the least of which is his satire of those who were seeking to apply the concepts of science to the art of politics. The distortions evident in their treatment of that discipline could only be increased as they were applied to the even more difficult art of poetry.

Against them, Tate offered a definition of poetry. It is, he said, "the art of apprehending and concentrating our experience in the mysterious limitations of form."[2] This definition, which shows the obvious influence of Hulme and Eliot, expresses his "reactionary" thesis by using a Latinate vocabulary suggestive of Classicism. He is explicitly anti-scientific and anti-romantic. But underneath he seems less certain. "Mysterious," in particular, makes a curious qualification. The Classicist stressed that part of man's experience and expression that is knowable. He agreed to keep within the limits of that part of experience accessible to the reason. But Tate's mind does not stop on the inside of those limits; rather it is looking on those limits from beyond. The result is that he looks at his limitations of form not with a truly Classical eye that can see no more than its Classicism, but with one that has chosen to see no more. Like Hulme and Eliot, he had seen beyond and could never quite return.

But their outlook is not without usefulness. It does diminish the force of the label these writers chose to affect, but they were too sophisticated to have believed that all of their experience could be contained in a few labels. These were merely useful in helping to establish a critical position. And far more important for the critic is his ability to find devices that will enable him to see deeply into the concrete expression of his age.

I *"Three Types of Poetry"*

In this first volume the essay "Three Types of Poetry" is noteworthy for its use of a critical method characteristic of Tate's best work. Essentially, his approach consists of demonstrating the importance of a problem of art by focusing it against a larger background. In so doing, the critic is forced to take account of the complexity of his problem; he cannot simplify it by reducing it to an immediate issue. In "Three Types of Poetry" Tate's subject has to do with poetry in the twentieth century. Yet he broadens the problem by referring it to the poetry of the Western world since Dante. In this respect his criticism is historical, a fact which might seem inconsistent in a man who has so often written about literary historians as men who have used the past without understanding it. But his use of history emphasizes his vantage point in the twentieth century: he assumes that the past forms an organic unity with the present. Because of the past's inseparability from the present, history can never for him become an object merely to be contemplated.

In "Three Types of Poetry," Tate's comparisons serve the purpose of illuminating certain problems which he feels are most compelling in twentieth-century poetry. These problems have to do with the impulses of mind which generate poetry: he classifies them as those stemming from the "practical will," those giving rise to "romantic irony," and those coming from the "creative spirit."[3] For illustrations of each type he goes to Dante, to Shelley, and to Shakespeare. He is careful to point out that he offers the three types as suggestive only, for there are many other kinds of poetry.

For Tate the most important category seems to be that of the "practical will"; it is the impulse which was so perfectly controlled in Dante. Presumably it still has great potential for arousing poetic creativity, but its disadvantage is that it has been badly distorted by modern science. Tate believes that the "practical will" was best controlled by the discipline of the method of allegory; this occurred in the period before the seventeenth century. Modern man, he says, cannot understand allegory as Dante employed it, for he can understand only fictional allegory. While Dante himself used fictional allegory, he was much more interested in religious allegory. In the last analysis, the demonstrable truth of the allegory in his poem enabled him to give greatness to his work. This was the "practical will" put to literary use. Though Tate does not dwell on the methods by which this approach may be brought into modern poetry, he obviously has little faith that modern man will be able to reconstitute the basis on which Dante's poetry was built.[4]

Looking forward from this vantage point toward the eighteenth century, Tate observes that the kind of make-believe allegory present in "Absalom and Achitophel" demonstrates that allegory was no longer being taken seriously.[5] And what was true of Dryden was doubly true of the Romantics. They simply forgot Dante's control of the "practical will" and allowed the will to assert itself wherever it would. The assertion of power, says Tate, was for the Romantic an absolute psychological necessity. Setting himself against the world, Shelley and others like him could attempt to assert their wills but in the process could hardly avoid ultimate disillusionment. And self-pitying sentimentality became their specialty. This quality represents all that Tate opposes. Even when he appraises a Romantic for whom he felt a personal fondness—Hart Crane—he expresses his disapprobation of the tendency to escape. Only in one Romantic poet, Rimbaud, does Tate find an artist with the ability to avert this danger. The Frenchman had the courage to see that he must either destroy his romantic will or escape from his poetry into action.[6]

Romanticism is defined as "science without the systematic method of asserting the will."[7] Tate hardly intends to be exhaustive; instead, he seems deliberately polemical and suggestive. By linking science, the arch-enemy of modern poetry, with the soft sentimentalities of Romanticism at its worst, he makes it much less formidable. The element of personification in his expression helps him to establish that the relationship between science and Romanticism is somewhat tentative and enigmatic, a condition which he chooses to explore by reference to a modern example.

In the work of I. A. Richards, Tate believes that both the scientific and Romantic impulses come together. Richards is a scientist, but at the same time, according to Tate, his "underlying assumption about poetry is like Mr. Edmund Wilson's, embedded in the humanitarian mentality of the age, where it lies too deep for examination."[8] What puts Richards into Tate's historical framework is his demand for an allegorical, utilitarian function for literature. This is the "practical will," with which poetry has been concerned since Dante. And undiluted interference of the will with poetry is precisely what Tate feels must be eliminated before genuine poetry can assume its place. For he believes that the "integral quality of the work of art forever resists practical formulation."[9]

The three types of poetry which he has under discussion finally lead to a formulation of a single criterion for poetry as an art. Behind the operation of history, he sees something more perdurable than anything in history. Even Dante's practice, he implies, does no more than offer the best approximation of poetic practice that we are likely to have. For poetry, he says, "finds its true usefulness in its perfect inutility."[10] So far as the ordinary affairs of life are concerned, poetry "proves nothing; it creates the totality of experience in its quality; and it has no useful relation to the ordinary forms of action."[11] But, lest these formulas tie him too closely to a theory of art for art's sake, he qualifies somewhat: "When the will and its formulas are put into an implicit relation with the whole of our experience, we get the true knowledge which is poetry."[12]

As an analysis of the poetic impulse, the essay is far from complete. Perhaps it is most profitable to regard it as an extended metaphor in which Tate willingly accepts the limitations of his expression in order to suggest much more. His opposition of the creative spirit and the scientific impulse seems excessively severe, especially by comparison with the generosity of a scientist such as Whitehead.[13] Though it is indeed true that the spirit of science is frequently overspecialized, not all scientists are so. By attributing this limitation to all of his adversaries, Tate courts the danger of seeming merely opinionated. Yet his argument, if not pushed too far, has merit.

The element of personification is a valuable device for giving tone to his essay. Clauses such as "the creative spirit occupies an aloof middle ground,"[14] or "about this fact science alone can instruct us"[15] give interest to his argument by their attribution of personality to prosaic abstractions. The reader feels along with Tate the force of the opposition of personalities which lead to these differing outlooks. But the emotional element in this device inevitably carries with it a certain imprecision, and it reduces the intellectual force of Tate's argument.

Particularly on the issue of freedom of the will, Tate's position seems less than satisfactory. Because he yields so much to the spirit of the age as the causative agent in the formation of the poet, he makes it hard to differentiate the poet from the scientist. Both, it would seem, are somewhat less than free agents. And of the two the scientist would seem the better able to afford a deterministic outlook. Perhaps this is true because he seems the more certain of the agent of change in the operation of the spirit of his age. Tate does not fully describe the nature of the agency for his poet; perhaps, like most conservative thinkers, he would fall back on an argument from the nature of man. But in the final analysis, he leaves this issue for his reader's conjecture.

But Tate's philosophical outlook is much less important for his criticism than are his examinations of the elements of poetic practice. His comparisons of the uses of allegory by various poets have lasting value for the study of poetry. His evaluations of the poetic practice of Dante, Shelley, and Arnold command attention for their cogency of reasoning. But perhaps his contribution comes most of all from a sincerity of expression stemming from his conviction of the value of poetic creation.

II *"Tension in Poetry"*

One of the most important of Tate's critical essays is "Tension in Poetry" (1938). Again and again it has proved itself useful to later critics, a fact which is perhaps some measure of its permanent value. Certainly, the issue that Tate explores is of enduring interest: he is investigating the poetic element in the nature of language itself. Underlying his investigation is an assumption not far from that of Emerson—that language itself is inherently poetic. Yet, unlike Emerson, Tate is not content to rely on history, real or imagined. Instead, he seeks to make an analysis that will separate the elements which are the fundamental constituents of language.

Tate chooses as his basic device an expression which describes for him the essential quality of poetry: the word "tension." He arrives at this expression by removing the prefixes from "intension" and "extension," terms usually employed in formal logic. By creating this special word, he implies the necessity for both qualities in poetic expression and at the same time shows that both qualities are inherently related.

The polarities which Tate's expression includes are those of the connotative and denotative qualities of language. "Good poetry," he says, "is a unity of all the meanings from the furthest extremes of intension and extension."[16] In order to prove his point, he examines a selection of verse which fails in its extreme of poverty of connotation and another which shows a lack of denotation. Each example reveals that the application of the opposite quality of language would effect improvement, and it is easy to feel that the generalization has merit.

But on closer examination it seems that Tate has stopped short of all that he might have said. For the great problem is how poetic language is made to differ from ordinary expression. What he seems to mean is that the poet must arrange words in contexts which will free them as much as possible from the limitations of ordinary speech and writing. While no doubt every use of every word has the potential of calling up all of the intension and extension within that word, the usual effect of contexts is to limit the ranges of both. For clarity of utterance, some such limitation is nearly mandatory, lest those using language be swept away in an ocean of meaning.

Tate is right, it would seem, in a relative sense. Poetry does employ much more of the meaning inherent in language than other forms of expression. But instead of stressing the fullness of poetic expression at this point in his essay, he concentrates on the failures within certain types of poetry. He finds in the romantic poet a tendency to failure in denotation and in the metaphysical poet a failure in connotation. It is easy to see that he prefers the metaphysical, and the force of his argument here amounts to a plea for an emphasis on intension in poetry. And surely the problem of how the poet manipulates the logical elements in his language is important. Tate's examples show that he is clearly right in stressing the complexity of meanings in poetic contexts. But the demonstration of such a generalization is extremely difficult, if not impossible.

In the closing section of his essay, Tate is at his best as he demonstrates some of the implications of his theory. He makes an analysis of three lines from *The Divine Comedy*, those in which Francesca tells Dante where she lives. Tate points out the excellence of her choice of a metaphor of pursuit when she is describing the relationship of the tributaries of the Po to the river itself. The personification of the Po identifies her with the river and enables the reader to see how this figure interprets her sin: she has become the sin. Dante's identification of the tributaries of the Po with the winds of lust is another especial merit of this canto. Particularly successful is the way in which this idea is suggested by the sound of the sibilants in Dante's line. Tate concludes: "The river is thus both a visual and an auditory image, and since Francesca is her sin and her sin is embodied in this image, we are entitled to say that it is a sin that we can both hear and see."[17]

By choosing such a seemingly insignificant part of Dante's poem and by demonstrating at great length the intellectual and emotional content of the lines, Tate demonstrates the incredible vastness of content possible in great poetry. Though many critics have asserted much the same thing, Tate's demonstration and proof have far more force than mere assertion. For his argument is founded on the complexity of human expression as a necessary corollary of the complexity of human experience. James, Proust, Joyce, Mann, Eliot, and many others had dramatized this condition; and criticism has investigated some of its problems. But Tate's brief essay encompasses so much that "ambiguity," "impurity," or "paradox" seem only special cases of his idea. Whether or not the criticism of the future will depend on Tate's expression remains to be seen, but that it will depend on the condition he sought to express seems a certainty.

III *"The Angelic Imagination"*

Tate's criticism during the 1940's and 1950's continued his long-standing emphasis on the full analysis of the literary work according to principles relevant to its structure. True, he did make an occasional foray into polemics. He wrote against the literary historians, who seemed to him to parade their ignorance of criticism. He examined the effects of the overemphasis on science in the colleges. He heaped scorn on the pseudo-science in courses in education and in sociology. But none of these constituted a new emphasis for him; each was only a reconfirmation of his commitment to things intellectual.

In this period, though, a new element did appear: Tate's vocabulary began to include more of the terms of Roman Catholicism—a natural consequence of his having been converted to that religion. But it is easily possible to overemphasize this aspect of change in his thought, for he seems never to have been inimical to Catholic thought and institutions. Indeed, it appears that his conversion was a logical outcome of his lifetime of devotion to the causes of conservatism and rationalism. Although it is important to emphasize the continuity of Tate's later thought with his earlier thought, he does in this period find an opportunity to re-emphasize his old position and to examine his ideas in new contexts. This quality of renewal lends especial interest to the essays of this period.

In his preface to *The Forlorn Demon* (1952) Tate explains that his title refers to Poe, the subject of two of the essays in the volume. But it is difficult not to feel that he is evoking an image of the twentieth-century artist as well. The adjective "forlorn" seems only too appropriate for the pose that the twentieth-century poet in his role as outcast must assume. Yet, if the Saxon adjective is mocking and ironical, the noun conceals layers of meaning extending back into ancient mythology. Poe, and perhaps his twentieth-century followers, may be a demon, but he is also a δαίμων and as such is akin to the divine.

Yet this figure may announce a writer grown more pessimistic than he had been in the 1920's and 1930's. He had indeed always been able to see faults in society, religion, and poetry. And he had not offered any hope for easy amelioration of the condition of man or of his institutions. But as his slashingly worded titles had announced, he had always actively sought a better society for the South or a better poetry for the country. He may have been a reactionary, but as he himself pointed out, he was asking for the most radical change that it is possible to make.

In *The Forlorn Demon* Tate has shifted his emphasis. He is dealing not so much with the question, "What should our literature become?" as with "What makes our literature what it is?" The two questions for Tate, the traditionalist, were always essentially related. But now it seems that a commitment to action is no longer possible and that he must now resign himself to explanation.

But Tate is too much aware of the sterility of the academic mind not to attempt to avoid it himself. He chooses in "The Angelic Imagination: Poe as God" the role of an amateur theologian, though "with some embarrassment."[18] This stance enables him to avoid the blindness of unalleviated scholarship or that of an extreme commitment to action. At the same time he can remove himself from some of the preciousness of formalist criticism. It was an approach for which Tate had evidently been preparing for some time: his enthusiastic footnotes to the work of Jacques and Raissa Maritain testify to his long-continued interest in their work.[19]

Tate's essential problem in "The Angelic Imagination" is of fundamental importance for twentieth-century criticism. On the surface his question is simple: Why does Poe seem so important to twentieth-century authors? Behind this question, though, is the admission of the meretriciousness of much of Poe's form. And for an age which has come close to elevating form into literature in its entirety, this amounts to an examination of the most fundamental assumptions behind the criticism of the age. If the interest in Poe is evoked by some quality in him that transcends his form, then perhaps the old vexed questions of form and matter cannot be so easily resolved as some twentieth-century critics have assumed. Though Tate does not make absolutely explicit all of these issues, they are implied in his question.

Tate's point of departure is T. S. Eliot's essay "From Poe to Valéry," the existence of which is proof almost enough in itself of the need of the twentieth-century critic to take Poe into account. The interesting point for Tate about Eliot's criticism is the elder critic's belief that Poe merely entertained his ideas. This statement would surely seem rash enough, and Tate counters that Poe could not have been insincere in all his ideas.

Tate believes that Poe was a religious man, "whose Christianity, for reasons that nobody knows anything about, had got short-circuited."[20] The argument needs to be examined, for it seems simply a way of trying to prove Poe's religiosity by calling attention to the absence of that quality. Perhaps Tate means to show that religious ideas were "in the air" in nineteenth-century America and that Poe could not have avoided their influence. If so, then his metaphor seems too strong for the kind of unconscious assimilation and rejection that might have taken place in Poe's mind. More than likely, Tate, the amateur theologian, is choosing the best theological ground on which to base his argument. His reasoning, therefore, has the force of metaphor—a mere aberration if wholly inappropriate or a potential source of insight if organic with its material.

Tate says that because Poe had no means of harmonizing the experience of the world, he became the victim of a hypertrophy of feeling, will, and intellect. And these qualities in Poe, Tate finds directly expressed in his works. But Tate is falling into the "intentional fallacy," for surely Poe may be granted the ability to imagine, as may any other author. Yet there is a sameness about Poe's characters, it may be granted, and perhaps there is a line of tendency in his writing that may somehow be related to Poe, the man.

The exaggeration of feeling in Poe's characters, Tate feels, "results in the loss of the entire natural order of experience."[21] And closely related to this idea is that of the hypertrophy of will, best exemplified in Poe's male characters, who so frequently violate the spiritual element of the female. But it is the third, or intellectual, perversion that most interests Tate. Discussing *The Conversation of Eiros and Charmion, The Colloquy of Monos and Una, The Power of Words,* and *Eureka,* he assigns them, as did Margaret Alterton, a central place in Poe's thought. He admits that Poe was merely ingenious rather than complex in his thought. But he grants that Poe had insight into the disintegration of personality, though he was at the same time a victim of that condition. Without fully comprehending the derangement of senses required for the presentation of synaesthesia, Poe came close to using that device in *The Colloquy of Monos and Una.* Yet he stopped short of actually feeling what he had intellectually proposed.

Tate explains Poe's failure as a natural one: "the discoverer of a new sensibility seldom pushes it as far as language will take it."[22] Poe used the traditional rhetoric because he feared the disorder which lurked beneath his language. Tate believes that Poe makes the transition to modern literature because he presents its characteristic subject matter, though "in a language that had developed in a tradition of unity and order."[23]

This split between Poe's ability consciously to manipulate his material and his ability to imagine is visible, Tate feels, in *The Conversation of Eiros and Charmion.* He believes that this is a "Cartesian split—taste, feeling, respect for the depth of nature, resolved into a subjectivism which denies the sensible world."[24]

From this dissociation of feeling and intellect can only result the hypertrophy of intellect and will. At this point Tate uses the authority of Maritain to show that exceeding the bounds of the human always results in "angelism." Tate believes that Poe surrendered to this condition entirely. And it is at this point that the argument shows most strain. The arguments of Tate and Maritain seem up to this point to offer useful metaphors with which to express the inclination of Poe's mind. But, when Tate presses his metaphor to the absolute, he comes close to reducing his argument to special pleading.

In his analysis of *The Power of Words*, Tate finds that Poe drove beyond the bounds of mere "angelism." The speakers in Poe's dialogue—angels themselves—have not only the knowledge of essences; they can create by means of words. This power, Tate says, is "superangelism"; this is man assuming the aspect of God in His creativity. Tate finds that Poe's giving his angels this attribute is a natural consequence of the hypertrophy of his own feeling, will, and intellect. But in this section he introduces a new idea: that the age is at least somewhat to blame for Poe's condition.[25] And this is a rather jarring blow. Before, he seemed sure that Poe's condition resulted from his choice as a religious man gone astray. To introduce incidentally the idea that Poe was determined by forces outside his control gives the reader the impression that Tate is not entirely certain in his own mind about his argument; it is evidence of some conflict in him between freedom of will and necessity.

Finally, Tate believes that Poe took a further step toward the maelstrom in *Eureka*, in which Poe was glorifying the omniscient intellect of man. Reaching forward toward the idea of the essential unity of the universe, this mind sees in the heart of that unity its own ultimate destruction. This is the image of the abyss, which, Tate believes, is in all of Poe's serious writings. The fact that Poe's thought led to this ultimate nothingness, the critic believes, was caused by the fact that he removed himself from the sensible world. Tate says that the human intellect "cannot reach God as essence; only God as analogy."[26]

There is a large measure of rightness in this argument. The only credible illusion the artist can create of man is that of a being radically imperfect. The hypertrophy of any of his qualities can only result in the emergence of a monster. It is probably true that Poe did not fully understand the effect of his distortion. But, seemingly, Poe should be criticized on the ground, not of his failure of moral vision, but of his failure as an artist.

Otherwise, Poe becomes merely a subject on which Tate can project his old thesis, in somewhat modified form, of the dissociated sensibility and intellect. What Tate needed for this essay was a somewhat more objective reason for applying this idea to Poe. It seems rather puzzling that he did not use the interpretation of the Virginian mind which he had advanced in *The Fathers*; the ante-bellum South gave many signs of a culture lag which caused it to hold to Neo-Classical values.[27] Poe's training at the University of Virginia would certainly have helped to give his mind a set in this direction. And because he so frequently aimed to please a public, it was easy enough for his mind to take the set toward rationalism that this culture lag would imply.

As for the image of the abyss, it would seem hardly to have been original with Poe. Certainly he would have found it in some form in the Calvinistic thought so characteristic of large segments of the population. Poe gave it his own interpretation, it is true, but Tate does not analyze what is distinctive about Poe's use of the image as opposed to that of others. Perhaps Tate might have looked more closely into the causative element in Western culture which gave the image to Jonathan Edwards, Baudelaire, and Tate himself.

Perhaps one of the greatest merits of Tate's essay is that it shows his open-minded willingness to attempt many kinds of criticism. There can be little question that Poe hardly merits so much of an important critic's attention. Yet he gives him the benefit of a prolonged hearing and a careful analysis. Even if Poe is only a kind of Ivan's devil to Tate, he receives a treatment that gives him more than a fair hearing.

IV *Final Estimate*

To try to give Tate his rightful place in twentieth-century criticism requires, no doubt, a longer perspective than is now available. For despite the gentlemanly tones of his work, he has always been a strongly polemical writer. His essays show the passionate concern he has felt for the issues under discussion, and they have not been without their opponents. Though much of what he has fought for has long been won, he is still somewhat a controversial figure.

His criticism is perhaps most valuable when he is discussing the nature of poetry. One of the characteristics of poetry that he has been more willing to emphasize than many critics is its seriousness of purpose. He may derive some of this emphasis from Arnold, but he seems more deeply philosophical than Arnold when he writes of "that fullness of actuality which we do not wholly understand, but which we require of poetry."[28] He does not attempt to describe actuality with any fullness, but it seems to be associated with concreteness, the unabstracted which accommodates the full range of complexity which must be contained in experience. For poetry's attempt to contain so much, it must be more philosophical than philosophy itself.

Another idea equally important to Tate is that of the importance of form. About this point Tate and others of his outlook came into conflict with those who felt that form can be separated from meaning—that form, while important, is not essential. For them an idea can be expressed in many different shapes; the manner of its presentation matters less than the idea itself. But for Tate, form is much more important. As he wrote in his essay on John Peale Bishop: "form is meaning and nothing but meaning."[29]

The consequences of this view are that Tate has been led to emphasize how the work of art is put together. For him, the distinctively literary quality of a poem, play, or novel is the manner of its presentation. As he writes in his essay on Longinus, "Style does not create the subject, it discovers it."[30] As a consequence, his literary essays devote much of their space to the analysis of particular elements of style. And in this area his essays make their greatest contribution—in the insights which the practicing poet shows into the process of creativity. Tate contends that for Shakespeare, "meaning is not in the content of his expression; it is in the tension of the dramatic relations of his characters."[31] His analysis of Emily Dickinson's "Because I Could not Stop for Death" provides analysis of language like this: "The sharp *gazing* before *grain* instills into nature a cold vitality of which the qualitative richness has infinite depth."[32] And his analysis of *The Idiot* yields: "The fly comes to stand in its sinister and abundant life for the privation of life, the body of the young woman on the bed."[33] With insights like these, Tate has helped to establish a climate of opinion in which they now seem inevitable.

The fact that his general critical outlook coincides with that of others has led to his being classified as a "New Critic" or as a "formalist critic." Neither epithet is more than a crude approximation of what he has been as a critic. He has always sought to return to first principles, and he has never emphasized form to the exclusion of other elements. When the controversies that gave rise to these epithets have vanished, his criticism will remain. Where he will rank is probably not even a very useful question, but he will be remembered as an important critic in an age which contributed much to criticism.

CHAPTER 9

The Major Phase

"S EASONS OF THE SOUL," Tate's largest and perhaps most important poem so far, is not so widely known as the "Ode to the Confederate Dead"; but it has had a sophisticated audience and has received discerning critical attention. Recently, it has been described as one of the most important poems of the twentieth century.[1] This judgment may overstate the case; certainly parts of *The Waste Land* seem more intensely realized. But, as Tate himself has remarked, the ascription of rank to poems probably contributes much less to criticism than the examination of the intrinsic qualities of the works themselves.

In this poem, Tate is at pains to create what Martin Foss has called the "metaphorical present."[2] This requirement is met by the use of a dramatic monologue in which the speaker addresses successively the personified seasons—summer, autumn, winter, and spring. But these seasons are in some sense parts of his own personality. His dialogue, then, is somewhat like the communication of the "I" with the "Thou" which Foss finds at the heart of expression.[3] The illusion which Tate is creating is indeed religious, as Mr. Meiners has suggested;[4] but it is deeper than the mere formulas of much religious expression. For, in giving his thought artistic form, Tate has touched the centers at which man is most free and therefore most human.

To achieve his artistic purpose, he establishes a speaker through whom the entire poem is focused and who is characterized entirely by the implications of his speech. He necessarily has carefully established this individual's mental perspective. In the "Ode to the Confederate Dead," the man at the cemetery had been stimulated by the symbolic force of what he found before him: he found the cemetery a part of a much larger whole. But if this attitude bespoke a largeness of mental possession, it also implied that the speaker himself was somewhat possessed by his symbol. As Foss has pointed out, the symbolic process always involves some reduction.[5] By contrast, the speaker in "Seasons of the Soul" is stimulated by the metaphorical. His meditation is set in motion by his understanding of the implications of the fall of France. The fact that this is metaphorical instead of symbolic process prevents his being mastered by his form. The speaker moves through the poem in the immediacy of the present. Whatever of his illusion is merely symbolic is transformed into the living process of metaphor.

I *"Summer"*

The speech of which the poem is comprised shows extreme simplicity of form. The short lines and frequent rhymes might seem appropriate only for the simplest subject matter; it is indicative of Tate's mastery of rhythm that they immediately establish themselves as entirely appropriate. By using strong variations on the basic iambic pattern, he gives his lines the unexpectedness suggestive of the surprising turns of mind of the intellectual. Yet the shortness of line and the predominantly masculine rhymes help to provide strength and definiteness. Theirs is the quality of the speech of a person accustomed to action instead of the passivity of mere meditativeness.

The poem opens with a rather formal address:

> Summer, this is our flesh,
> The body you let mature;
> If now while the body is fresh
> You take it, shall we give
> The heart, lest heart endure
> The mind's tattering
> Blow of greedy claws?[6]

The contrast between the promise of the season and the offer of religious sacrifice implied in the figure of "flesh" sets an ironical tone. And the emphasis of the rhyming word "fresh" focuses attention on the possibility of decay. This season appropriately expresses the condition of the twentieth century in that its external beauty is marred by internal rot. And the cause is the one emphasized by Tate in so many of his earlier works: the split between the sensibility and the intellect. The representation of this idea in a cat figure shows the greed, the lawless individualism, and the horror at the soul of modern man. For the mind, as apart from the sensibility, the speaker apparently has little hope.

His reversal of the cat figure, beginning in line eight, amplifies his feeling: "Shall mind itself still live/If like a hunting king/ It falls to the lion's jaws?" With the tentativeness of simile, he uses the king to bring to mind all the better qualities of the human intellect in responsible action. And he emphasizes the need for discipline by the adjective "hunting," which has to do with stylized ritual. This is a good way of concentrating and controlling emotion, but the twentieth century has very nearly lost its sense of the value of convention. The inability of the men of the twentieth century to find a way of integrating sensibility and intellect as this hypothetical king might do is the fundamental problem against which the poem is set.

In the second stanza the speaker's tones become harsher as he turns to the prophetic:

> Under the summer's blast
> The soul cannot endure
> Unless by sleight or fast
> It seize or deny its day
> To make the eye secure.

The reason, conceived of as excessive energy received from the sun, is opposed to the sensibility, now spoken of as "soul." In a world dominated by the mere intellect, only cunning or renunciation can insure the retention of spiritual values. Yet, by using the eye as a symbol of the soul, the speaker is able to show how ironical is the achievement of safety through deprivation. Security from excess of reason is purchased only at the cost of the soul's nutriment. Even this is preferable to the consequences for those who deny the reason entirely. In the address to his "brothers-in-arms," beginning with line sixteen, he calls attention to the hot wind which

> ... dries and draws
> With circular delay
> The flesh, ash from the ember,
> Into the summer's jaws.

The speaker is recalling the punishment of those in the second circle of the Inferno, with its whirling winds that punish the incontinent. And by using the Christian symbols of flesh, ash, and ember, he makes more explicit Dante's values. To them, he implies, the spiritual problems of modern man must be referred.

The next stanza gives an example of the deceptiveness of appearances in such a world. The solstice, like Eliot's "zero summer,"[7] brings to mind the idea of balance; and it may imply the choice of good and evil in Eden. This inference leads the speaker to think of "green" France, an adjective which associates her with the naïveté and fertility of the Garden. The caterpillar is a lesser serpent. "Caterpillar feet" bring to mind the mechanism of the tank treads as well as the sexual symbolism of the tramping feet of the army. All of these images add up to an interpretation of the fall of France as a second Fall, and the reasons for both are essentially the same. Man's overemphasis on the intellect, apart from the sensibility, allows him to live in a partial and imperfect view of his condition.

The homelessness of men dispossessed by war is reminiscent of those cursed in Eden. The description of the claws of war as "usurping" links the cat figure of the reason, individualism, and evil with original sin conceived of as a function of the intellect dissociated from the sensibility. The legal term "escheat" brings up the possibility of the loss of man's entire estate because of his failure to provide the proper conditions for the development of the sensibility. This heart of man is described as a "green field" because it may still achieve the condition it had in Eden. And it is particularly ironic that the speaker must under the present conditions call it "meat for the weevil," in a reference that implies the insidiousness and uncleanness of man's sin.

In the fourth stanza the tension of the verse begins to relax as, ironically, the promise of summer moves over toward the stillness of death:

> The southern summer dies
> Evenly in the fall:
> We raise our tired eyes
> Into a sky of glass.

"Fall" signifies not only the end of summer but, as has been noted, the fall of France and the Fall in Eden. The eyes of men, tired of the harshness of the realities below, escape into a world like that of Shelley's inane simile of the "dome of many colored glass." This world, though, is merely idealized space, "blue, empty, and tall." It has no form; all ethereal, it does not, the speaker feels, permit of the head and the tail of the devil. In this place, the fact that the laws "burn" means that they have a meretricious quality, especially since they are the same for Balaam and his ass. And that these things take place above the "invalid" dead is ironical, for the dead do alter the context of every man's experience. Though they cannot lift their jaws to take action, they do speak by their having been—by the fact that they help to constitute history and that they make up a part of the memory of man.

This thought of the past turns the mind of the speaker to the question:

> When was it that the summer
> (Daylong a liquid light)
> And a child, the new-comer,
> Bathed in the same green spray,
> Could neither guess the night?

During this time when a primitive vegetation religion was current, summer symbolized what was emotionally close to man; the figure of light suggests its ministration to his spirit. The child, here associated with the summer, seems like the corn-daughters described in Frazer's account of these ceremonies.[8] She symbolizes the vitality of the land, and she has a mystical identity with the season. Both, "bathed in the same green spray," experience the fufillment of the season—nature, literally; and the corn-daughter, with her wrapping of leaves signifying her identity with nature, metaphorically. Neither can "guess the night" because each lives according to the organic time of nature. But, as the latter part of the stanza denotes, this "time-less day" passed into an age more conscious of mechanical time. This awareness shows the influence of positivism, which is the agent that has caused the speaker and his age along with him to be trapped in "time's engaging jaws."

In the last stanza of this section the speaker advances an idea which provides the means of disengagement from time—a retreat into the timeless in an experience such as that of Dante. In the speaker's view, Dante and Virgil had a positive identity as they began their errand: they were like "men of our summer world." But as they retreated further from the time-order on which they were dependent, their "shadows curled." That is, they were faced with loss of identity, and as a result they "fearfully confounded/The vast concluding shell." At this point in their journey, the need for identity is demonstrated in the actions of the wise centaur Chiron.

His bringing up the problem of identity makes the speaker realize that this is a central difficulty for him and for his age. His positivistic emphasis on the intellect should have enabled him to know himself, for he might seem to be able to make himself the object of his own contemplation. But the actions of Chiron make it evident that he may be able to know, but not to understand. To his problem he must bring the full sensibility. The possibility of his doing so is the unresolved issue that anticipates the "Autumn" section of the poem.

II *"Autumn"*

Without any alteration in the basic metrical pattern of the utterance, the speaker shifts his tone so as to make a more positive emphasis on the possibility of action. The latent energy of his trimeters is brought out by a predominantly monosyllabic vocabulary. It is as if the speaker has caught a fresh breath of resolve and is ready to impart a fresh perspective to his problem.

In this section he uses a dream psychology to suggest the unreal quality of this autumnal world: "It had an autumn smell/ And that was how I knew/That I was down a well." The context in which the speaker finds himself makes all the difference: "an autumn smell" might connote a sentimentally pleasant sensation granted the right surroundings. But here the well ironically reflects back unpleasant overtones upon it. The well might be out of *Alice in Wonderland,* and it emphasizes the sexual symbolism in the modern consciousness. This is simply a part of twentieth-century emphasis on determinism. The speaker looks on his age as a trap, and he even grows self-pitying: "My lips were numb and blue." At the end of the section the unreality

of his surroundings receives further emphasis. He makes a
magician's gesture, and his world is turned ninety degrees; he
is now trapped in a hall instead of a well.

There is more than a hint of Kafka in the description of
the hall. The words tell much about the condition of the speaker's unconscious mind: "The round ceiling was high/And the
gray light like shale/Thin, crumbling, and dry." This comparison
of his mind with the interior of a church implies the speaker's
awareness of the possibility of his own spiritual elevation. But at
the same time, the simile undercuts this idea by reminding him
of his kinship with the mineral. And later in the same stanza,
he speaks of the doors opening into the hall as potentially the
places where ghosts might be admitted. Together, his figures
represent the speaker's full awareness of his own involvement
in the dehumanization of modern man.

This awareness produces reaction, and in the third stanza
the speaker expresses his wish for escape from his terrible
individualism:

> I will leave this house, I said,
> There is the autumn weather—
> Here, nor living nor dead;
> The lights burn in the town
> Where men fear together.

Yet the possibility of escape only makes him aware of the
futility of escape. The men outside pay little attention to the
"fine autumn weather," for they, too, are victims of the locked-in
ego. Like the people of *The Waste Land*, they are neither "living
nor dead"; they "fear together."

The thought of the men causes him to make a further gesture:

> Then on the bare floor,
> But tiptoe lest I fall,
> I walked years down
> Towards the front door
> At the end of the empty hall.

This action indicates the strain that the speaker must undergo
to find his identity. Its secretiveness stresses the individualism
that causes him to fear the arousal of any of his ghosts. He has
need to be careful, for he is in effect trying to find himself by

reversing his own development, by telescoping the past into the present.

Like one of Kafka's heroes, the speaker finds that the door is false. He is imprisoned not even by the mechanical (and sexual) agency of key and lock, but by his own illusion. Yet he describes himself as "caught" in the house, a term which implies guilt and perhaps self-pity. This feeling is perhaps deepened by his saying that he was "born to it," implying his awareness that this house is indeed a part of himself. And this idea is made all the more ironical by the lines: "For miles of running brought/Me back where I began." He is becoming fully aware of the likeness to a squirrel cage of modern man's effort to integrate his sensibility with his intellect.

Again like a Kafka hero, the speaker meets his father at this crucial moment. This meeting is described in an elaborate simile which suggests at once the importance of the encounter and its distance from ordinary reality:

> As in a moonlit street
> Men meeting are too shy
> To check their hurried feet
> But raise their eyes and squint
> As through a needle's eye
> Into the faceless gloom.

The street, the needle's eye, and the "faceless gloom" express the determinism which is at base the difficulty of the speaker, as well as of his contemporaries. The hurrying feet and squinting eyes are effects which result from the shyness brought on by his realization of the force of this all-enveloping determinism. Yet the father as the chief directing force of the son's life does not identify himself with his son. And all the others whom he has known fail to recognize him, even though they have helped to make his identity.

The final lines of the "Autumn" section place the blame on "him whose vision froze/Him in the empty hall." Here the word "vision" brings the failure home to the intellect of the speaker himself. As the "Summer" section represents the external side of this modern problem, the "Autumn" represents the internal. The stylization of its subject matter distances the emotion from the merely personal; this is particularly necessary because of the element of self-pity engendered by his determinism. Within the limits of the Kafka-like figures in which his mind can work, the speaker comes to know himself. He is ready to accept blame for that part of himself which is responsible for his failure and for that of his age. Having arrived at this stage of self-awareness, he is ready for the more active qualities he displays in the next section.

III   "Winter"

The change in movement in this section is appropriate to the symphonic structure of the work: this is prayer, perhaps the most appropriate utterance for winter. It is addressed to Venus:

> Goddess sea-born and bright,
> Return into the sea
> Where eddying twilight
> Gathers upon your people—
> Cold goddess, hear our plea!

This prayer seems to call on Venus in her later character as Venus Geneatrix more than in her quality as the goddess of love. This emphasis is especially evident in the final line of each section: "living wound of love." If the joy-pain relationship is here implied, the accent is clearly on pain.

The reason is not far to seek. The picture of the modern world which this prayer evokes is one of desolation. The "burst earth" has no joy for its inhabitants, and they are bathed in "eddying twilight." Their God has failed: akin to the Hanged Man of Frazer, he is desiccated and impotent. The prayer to Venus, then, is for relief from the curse which this impotence has brought upon the land. Yet it is clear that the speaker is not literally thinking of the conditions described in the "Summer" section so much as those of "Autumn." The plea to Venus is ultimately a plea for a renewal of values—for a reconstitution of the unconscious mind.

In the second stanza the speaker makes the plea for Venus to "come home/To your salt maidenhead." Here the figure of the salt implies "essential element," and it associates Venus with all the constructive values of his universe. But, in the

"Ode to the Confederate Dead," salt had been used to emphasize the somewhat poisonous element in life itself, and so is it used here. Life and death are closely associated. The force of this idea is amplified in his personifications "anonymous sea" and "shuddering foam." Though the sea provides a "shade for lovers," in the depths lurks the shark. The speaker contrasts it with the dove of Venus, but in so doing shows how these opposites must be a part of the same unity.

The third stanza makes explicit the speaker's use of the sea as a figure for the mind:

> And now the winter sea:
> Within her hollow rind
> What sleek facility
> Of sea-conceited scop
> To plumb the nether mind!

By this ironic mockery of the limitations of the figure, the speaker points up the need for expansion of his vision—a need which he supplies in the second half of his stanza:

> Eternal winters blow
> Shivering flakes, and shove
> Bodies that wheel and drop—
> Cold soot upon the snow
> Their livid wound of love.

The use of the weather suggests the forces of the external world which must impinge upon individual men. The participle "shivering" helps to personify "flakes," which are associated with the individuals determined by a world full of forces beyond their control. In this world, winters "shove" men to their doom. As they go, they describe the figure of a wheel, in which the possibility of the free flight of the bird is ironically tightened into the figure of a wheel indicative of determinism. And when they rest finally as "Cold soot upon the snow," they are entirely alienated from the universe. Its icy purity contrasts absolutely with the impurity of man himself.

With the section beginning "Beyond the undertow," the speaker seeks an emotional resolution for this problem of determinism, which he recognizes as one of the most compelling forces in his universe. He examines the "gray sea-foliage," which implies a kind of fecundity. Yet its color seems anything but that of the color of the hair of Whitman's graves. Its tangled condition and its meager illumination ("phosphor glow") suggest the feebleness of intellect and the strong dependence on determinism that might be supposed to operate at so great a remove from the heart of light. That this is a sea jungle is emphasized by the device of *montage*. The speaker turns suddenly back to his cat figure. In his picture of this animal preening itself for the act of "love," he returns once more to his theme of the selfishness of individualism incapable of love.

In the final stanza in the "Winter" section, the speaker looks again "beyond the undertow." He uses this time the madripore, or reef-building coral, as a way of suggesting perhaps the existence of a self-generating element in nature. If it can assert its own will against all the elements, then perhaps it illustrates the operation of an elemental principle in man as well. But the figure also suggests the rigidity of death. The speaker's longing for life causes him to make another comparison of the madripore with a "Headless, unageing oak/That gives the leaf no more." There is a lingering vestige of the Romantic in this figure: a Werther could have found in it the basis for endless self-pity.

But the mind of this speaker is led to that part of Dante's Hell referred to in the epigraph to the poem. He is in the seventh circle among those violent against themselves. The blood which springs from the broken branch of the tree speaks to him, as it did to Dante. The speakers identify themselves as "Lovers whose stratagem/Led to their suicide." Then he finds his own hair wet with blood and understands that he, too, is one of them. This is his baptism.

This section, then, ends on the psychological climax of the poem. It began in the speaker's ability to pray, for which he had been prepared by the experience of thoughtful contemplation in the "Summer" and "Autumn" sections of the poem. But the sterility of mere knowledge was overcome by the call for action which is prayer. In the course of that prayer, he comes to understand himself. Having undergone the symbolic cleansing of baptism, he is stripped of pride and ready to admit that he also is "maimed." With this spirit he is perhaps ready for regeneration.

IV *"Spring"*

The whole of "Spring" is suffused with the contrition which the speaker had experienced in "Winter." But he is too sophisticated to believe that regeneration can come easily, and for this reason he cannot feel immediately the joy which might be felt by the naïve. Regeneration is for him an ordeal, a responsibility which he must accept in tones as complex as those in which he originally comprehended his problem. Ultimately, he must find within himself the spiritual force to accept his own individual extinction in something larger than himself. This path from self-knowledge to the extinction of pride of will is traced in this section.

The speaker's choice of vocabulary renders very well the illusion of his state of mind. His use of "irritable" to qualify "spring" has an ironic quality which helps to associate this season with that of *The Waste Land* and *Murder in the Cathedral*. Its Latinate quality causes the adjective to carry—concealed, perhaps—some of the overtones it had in the earlier language. One of these senses is "provocative of love." By means of this expression, the speaker is able to bring up the joy-pain relationship and to reinterpret it with the irony necessary for the modern sensibility. Likewise, the verb "infuse" depends somewhat upon the overtones it had in Late Latin; it therefore means "melting" as well as "pour into." And the same technique must be applied to "combustible," which assimilates some of the figurative meanings of the Latin *comburo*. Among these is Propertius' "to consume by love." And the word "liquid" suggests the idea of "clear."

All of these ideas coalesce to form an elaborate figure which explains love as an illuminating but consuming inhabitant of the body. Instead of being a part of the body, it is merely the "body's guest." This profoundly pessimistic interpretation of the soul's function is emphasized by the figure of the "dying coal." The effect of the first stanza of this section, therefore, is to invert the romantic picture of spring and love. Instead of perpetual renewal, they must bring to mind ultimate silence and death.

In the second stanza, the speaker turns back to the hopefulness

of his youth as a way of emphasizing the despair of his present
view of the world:

> Back in my native prime
> I saw the orient corn
> All space but no time,
> Reaching for the sun
> Of the land where I was born.

Like the ancients, he, too, had a mystical view of the renewal
of the earth. The resplendent corn he personified as he did
the sun, and he could speak of a nearly personal relationship
between himself and the land. In such a relationship he could
be reconciled even to death, which he interpreted as an organic
part of the life process. But this vision was "all space but no
time." Now he was in common with other men of his age the
positivist's preoccupation with time. And this reduction of every
part of life to mere time has blighted that land and this spring.

The repetition of the word "time" in the first sentence of
the third stanza (a repetition which recalls "The Love Song
of J. Alfred Prufrock") serves to re-emphasize the problem of
positivism:

> In time of bloody war
> Who will know the time?
> Is it a new spring star
> Within the timing chill,
> Talking, or just a mime,
> That rises in the blood—
> Thin Jack-and-Jilling seas
> Without the human will?

In this stanza the romantic vision of youth is brought forward
and reinterpreted. It is still possible for the speaker to imagine
a star as controlling his destiny, but the illusion soon fades into
the figures of the mime and of "Jack-and-Jilling seas." The
processes of the universe which once seemed so real now seem
divorced from human understanding. His play on the word
"time" shows that he attributes this condition to the positivist's
preoccupation with mechanical time, as opposed to the self-
renewing time of the organic universe. And this play on the
word "time" shows that this mechanical universe is alien to

him. He completes this part of his picture by reinterpreting the star of his romantic illusion as the sun, symbolic here as in "The Rime of the Ancient Mariner" of the reason.

In the following stanza, the speaker associates the sun with the "burning arrogance" in the soul of man. And he puts together Plato's myth of the cave and the myth of Sisyphus to re-emphasize and re-interpret man's preoccupation with shadows and his masochistic endeavor to raise a burden too great for him. The plea he addresses to Sisyphus, "Cover the cave's egress/Where light reveals the slave," shows his realization that the light of reason perverted is the source of man's being misled.

The closed cave brings to his mind other myths, especially that of the Seven Sleepers of the Koran: "Come, old woman, save/Your sons who have gone down/Into the burning cave." That the cave is "burning" is a reminder of the period of gestation through which they must go to be reborn. The speaker is calling upon the Earth-mother for protection and for renewal. He then shifts his figure to that of the Virgin Mary, and his tones grow more supplicating. These lead to his final stanza in which he confesses the fear which is at the center of his motives:

> Regard us, while the eye
> Discerns by sight or guess
> Whether, as sheep foregather
> Upon their crooked knees,
> We have begun to die.

The speaker is no longer arrogant: he has ceased to depend on the power of reason. He has cast off his faith in individualism and now sees himself as only one of a flock of sheep. Their knees are "crooked," not self-sufficient. They are resigned to extinction in an entity larger than themselves. And his resignation is perhaps as far as man can go.

V Conclusion and Estimate

Tate's poem is essentially a metaphor of twentieth-century man's spiritual condition. His interpretation, at once simple and complex, relies on the "split sensibility" thesis which has formed the basis for his interpretation of the condition of twentieth-century man for most of his career. Though this idea has the great merit of suggesting much about the heart of the twentieth-century outlook, it is probably a vast simplification. But it gives Tate an emotional center for his poem, and it enables him to give his work controlling form.

If the "split sensibility" thesis is the warp of the poem giving it shape and continuity, then the woof is provided by the "tension" of the words he employs. By his choice of words he expresses and controls the unbelievable complexity which is at the center of modern man's life. It is this complexity which makes it necessary that Tate's poem be difficult. It is this complexity that makes the rhythms of Tate's poem so different from those of poets unaware of the need to express so much.

In short, Tate has expressed his age in "Seasons of the Soul." He is not himself spiritually at one with the age, and this makes his task difficult. But his is only the task of every man of his epoch, and it helps to provide the essential tone of the time. That Tate has rendered the subject matter of his age in its own essential tones and rhythms is his great accomplishment in this poem.

CHAPTER 10

Prospects

A STUDY of a living author must always be tentative in its estimates, for the shape of a career cannot be known with any certainty until it can be seen in perspective. Each succeeding work in some degree reshapes the whole. For the fully developed artist, the works of the latter part of his career may even be his best. What would the reputation of Cervantes be like without the second part of *Don Quixote*, or of Beethoven without the Late Quartets, or of Dostoevsky without *The Brothers Karamazov*? Because Tate never depended on an early flowering of romantic emotion for his poetic force, he has been able to continue writing with his powers unimpaired. There is every reason to believe that he will continue to develop.

Though Tate has not published so much in recent years as formerly, he has a long poem in preparation. It is of course impossible at this time to assess the quality of this poem, but some of his recently published poems may give some indication of what it promises. "The Swimmers," which will presumably be one of the sections of the poem, has a much more personal tone than anything Tate has written previously. Its setting is "Montgomery County, Kentucky"; and it takes place in July, 1911.[1] One of the persons depicted is Tate himself as the boy of twelve that he would have been at that time. The experience described seems a personal one: the discovery of a lynched Negro. The use of narrative for the direct confrontation of experience had occurred in his poetry only infrequently before.

More than most of his earlier poetry, this poem depends on the evocation of sharply realized pictures. Those of the boys, the posse, the sheriff, and the Negro all have some symbolic force. But that of the hanged Negro is made explicitly in terms of Christ. The boy's understanding from this comparison of the guilt which he shares with all his town forms the ironic conclusion to the poem.

This new quality in Tate's poetry gives promise of a roundness and complexity that may excel anything he has created before. The great problem, it seems, would lie in the context he can establish for his narrative sections. In some way, the poet of the twentieth century must relate his material to the complexity which is the hallmark of our age. Otherwise, he can only seem escapist. But Tate has been nothing if not philosophically aware, and it seems a virtual certainty that he will establish a context that will enable him to achieve his most significant contribution to poetry.

Tate's place in American letters is secure. He is one of a very small number of American writers who have had the ability to present the intellectual as well as the emotional side of the American experience. In a culture which has seemed so often to encourage and even to depend on the anti-intellectual, he has emphasized the opposite. Ultimately, I feel, he will be proved to have dealt with the truly significant elements in our experience. For if the American has stumbled sometimes blindly with the load of all his society on his back, he has been groping toward the life of reason for all his number. His dimly realized ideal may yet succeed, and if it does it will be in large part because of those who prodded him forward so relentlessly—men like Allen Tate.

Notes and References

Chapter One

1. "Narcissus as Narcissus," *Collected Essays* (Denver, 1959), p. 248.
2. *Prejudices: Second Series* (New York, 1920), pp. 136-37.
3. Fred A. Shannon, *The Farmer's Last Frontier* (New York, 1945), p. 415.
4. Louise Cowan, *The Fugitive Group: A Literary History* (Baton Rouge, 1959), pp. 29ff.
5. *Ibid.*, pp. 44-48.
6. *Ibid.*, pp. 45-48.
7. *The Fugitive*, I (April, 1922), 9.
8. "The Artist and Society," *7 Arts*, ed. Fernando Puma (New York, 1953), p. 2.
9. *The Fugitive*, I (June, 1922), 39.
10. See *Oeuvres Complètes de Baudelaire*, ed. Claude Pichois (Tours, 1961), pp. 262-63.
11. *The Fugitive*, I (June, 1922), 57.
12. *The Fugitive*, I (October, 1922), 76.
13. See Cowan, p. 109.
14. *The Anatomy of Criticism* (Princeton, 1957), p. 17.
15. *The Fugitive*, I (December, 1922), 116-17.
16. Cowan, p. 130.
17. *The Fugitive*, II (June-July, 1923), 70-71.
18. *The Jade*, III (November 12, 1921), 17.
19. *The Fugitive*, III (February, 1924), 8.

Chapter Two

1. "One Escape from the Dilemma," *The Fugitive*, III (April, 1924), 34.
2. *Ibid.*, p. 35.
3. *Ibid.*
4. *Ibid.*
5. *Ibid.*, p. 36.
6. "Rhetoric, Mysticism, Poetry," *New Republic*, XLIV (October 14, 1925), 209.
7. *Ibid.*, p. 210.
8. "A Poetry of Ideas," *New Republic*, XLVII (June 30, 1926), 172.
9. T. S. Eliot, "The Function of Criticism," *Selected Essays* (New York, 1960), p. 14.
10. "A Poetry of Ideas," p. 172.
11. *Ibid.*
12. *Ibid.*

13. *Ibid.,* p. 173.
14. R. G. Collingwood, *The Idea of History* (New York, 1956), p. 181.
15. *Nation,* CXXII (May 12, 1926), 532-34.
16. *Nation,* CXXI (October 28, 1925), 485.
17. Cowan, p. 36.
18. "The Revolt Against Literature," *New Republic,* XLIX (February 9, 1927), 329-30.
19. "American Poetry Since 1920," *Bookman,* XLVIII (November, 1928), 504.
20. *Ibid.,* p. 507.

Chapter Three

1. Leon Edel, *Literary Biography,* (Toronto, 1957), p. 40.
2. *Stonewall Jackson: The Good Soldier* (Ann Arbor, 1960), p. 12.
3. Harold Underwood Faulkner, *American Economic History* (New York, 1949), p. 259.
4. *Stonewall Jackson,* p. 25.
5. Marie-Henri Beyle, *The Charterhouse of Parma,* trans. C. K. Scott-Moncrieff (Garden City, N. Y., 1953), p. 46.
6. *Stonewall Jackson,* p. 91.
7. *Ibid.,* p. 69.
8. *Ibid.,* p. 4.
9. *Ibid.,* p. 32.
10. *Ibid.,* p. 33.
11. *Ibid.,* p. 34.
12. *Ibid.,* p. 63.
13. *Ibid.,* pp. 83-86.
14. *Ibid.,* p. 87.
15. *Ibid.,* p. 13.
16. *Jefferson Davis: His Rise and Fall* (New York, 1929), p. 7.
17. *Ibid.*
18. *Ibid.,* pp. 7-8.
19. *Ibid.,* p. 65.
20. *Ibid.,* p. 68.
21. *Ibid.*
22. *Ibid.,* p. 127.
23. *Ibid.,* p. 132.
24. *Ibid.,* p. 197.
25. *Ibid.,* p. 251.
26. *Stonewall Jackson,* p. 272.

Chapter Four

1. Cowan, p. 149.
2. *Poems* (Denver, 1961), p. 138. This edition is like that of 1928 except that it substitutes "For" in the fourth line for "And," and that it makes a few changes in punctuation.
3. Cf. "Narcissus as Narcissus," *Collected Essays,* p. 251.

4. *Collected Essays*, p. 459.
5. Cf. *The Waste Land*, l. 60 and Eliot's note.
6. Cf. Tate's analysis of a similar symbol in *Collected Essays*, p. 255.
7. *Poems*, p. 109. This poem is unchanged from the 1928 version.
8. *Mr. Pope and Other Poems* (New York, 1928), pp. 41-42.
9. *Ibid.*, p. 43. The latest version of the poem is in *Poems*, p. 139.
10. *Mr. Pope and Other Poems*, p. 52. The latest version in *Poems* incorporates four changes in wording from the 1928 version.
11. "The Angelic Imagination: Poe as God," *Collected Essays*, p. 439.

Chapter Five

1. *I'll Take My Stand: The South and the Agrarian Tradition* (New York, 1930), p. 155.
2. *Ibid.*, p. xiv.
3. *Ibid.*, p. xix.
4. See his letter to James Madison of December 20, 1787, in *Alexander Hamilton and Thomas Jefferson: Representative Selections*, ed. F. C. Prescott (New York, 1934), pp. 262-69.
5. John D. Hicks, *The Populist Revolt* (Minneapolis, 1931), *passim.*
6. *The Octopus*, ed. Kenneth S. Lynn (Boston, 1958), pp. 395-96.
7. *Who Owns America? A New Declaration of Independence* (Boston, 1936), pp. 80-83.
8. *Ibid.*, pp. 82-87.
9. "Remarks on the Southern Religion," *I'll Take My Stand*, pp. 157-59.
10. *Ibid.*, pp. 160-66.
11. *Ibid.*, pp. 169-73.
12. *Ibid.*, p. 174.

Chapter Six

1. *Selected Poems* (New York, 1937), p. ix.
2. "Narcissus as Narcissus," *Collected Essays*, p. 250.
3. *Mr. Pope and Other Poems*, p. 33.
4. *Poems*, p. 19.
5. *Ibid.*, pp. 46-47.
6. *The Charterhouse of Parma*, p. 9.
7. *Poems*, pp. 166-72.
8. *Selected Essays* (New York, 1960), p. 5.

Chapter Seven

1. *Saturday Review of Literature*, XVIII (September 24, 1938), 6-7.
2. Mina Curtiss, "Period Piece," *Nation*, CXLVII (October 8, 1938), 358.
3. *Booklist*, XXXV (October 1, 1938), 49.
4. *New Republic*, XCVII (November 9, 1938), 25.
5. *Accent*, VII (1947), 101-9.

6. *The Art of the Novel: Critical Prefaces,* ed. R. P. Blackmur (New York. 1934), p. 320.

7. See *Poetics* 8.

8. "Swann's Way," *Remembrance of Things Past,* trans. C. K. Scott-Moncrieff (New York, 1934), I, 34-36.

9. *The Fathers* (Denver, 1961), p. 3.

10. "Hamlet and his Problems," *Selected Essays,* pp. 124-25.

11. *Collected Essays,* p. 408.

12. *Ibid.*

13. *The Fathers,* p. 131.

14. *Ibid.,* p. 272.

15. *Ibid.,* p. 22.

16. *Symbol and Metaphor in Human Experience* (Lincoln, n. d.), p. 13.

17. *The Fathers,* p. 125.

18. *Ibid.,* pp. 17-18.

19. *Ibid.,* p. 127.

20. *Ibid..* p. 38.

21. See "Romanticism and Classicism," *Criticism: the Foundations of Modern Literary Judgment,* ed. Mark Schorer, Josephine Miles, and Gordon McKenzie (New York, 1948), pp. 258-59.

22. *Selected Essays,* p. 32.

23. *The Fathers,* p. 54.

24. *Ibid.,* p. 227.

25. *Ibid.,* p. 258.

Chapter Eight

1. *Collected Essays,* p. xiv.

2. *Ibid.,* p. xv.

3. *Ibid.,* p. 91.

4. *Ibid.,* pp. 95-99.

5. *Ibid.,* p. 99.

6. *Ibid.,* pp. 100-5.

7. *Ibid.,* p. 100.

8. *Ibid.,* p. 108.

9. *Ibid.,* p. 111.

10. *Ibid..* p. 113.

11. *Ibid.*

12. *Ibid.*

13. See, for example, *The Aims of Education and Other Essays* (New York, 1952), pp. 67-68.

14. *Collected Essays,* p. 95.

15. *Ibid.*

16. *Ibid.,* p. 82.

17. *Ibid.,* p. 90.

18. *Ibid.,* p. 432.

19. *Ibid.,* p. 443n.

20. *Ibid.,* p. 433.

21. *Ibid.,* p. 434.

22. *Ibid.,* p. 438.
23. *Ibid.,* p. 439.
24. *Ibid.,* p. 442.
25. *Ibid.,* pp. 447-50.
26. *Ibid.,* p. 453.
27. See, for example, *The Fathers,* pp. 17-18.
28. *Collected Essays,* p. 427.
29. *Ibid.,* p. 240.
30. *Ibid..* p. 516.
31. *Ibid.,* p. 210.
32. *Ibid.,* p. 206.
33. *Ibid.,* p. 158.

Chapter Nine

1. R. K. Meiners, *The Last Alternatives: A Study of the Works of Allen Tate* (Denver, 1963), p. 154.
2. *Symbol and Metaphor,* pp. 108-11.
3. *Ibid.,* pp. 74-77.
4. *The Last Alternatives,* p. 155.
5. *Symbol and Metaphor,* pp. 13-33.
6. *Poems,* pp. 27-39.
7. "Little Gidding," *The Complete Poems and Plays, 1909-1950* (New York, 1962), p. 138.
8. *The Golden Bough* (New York, 1935), VII, 207-13.

Chapter Ten

1. *Poems,* pp. 175-79.

Selected Bibliography

PRIMARY SOURCES

A. *Books*

The Golden Mean and Other Poems. Tate and Ridley Wills. Nashville: Privately printed, 1923.

Stonewall Jackson: The Good Soldier. New York: Minton, Balch and Co., 1928.

Mr. Pope and Other Poems. New York: Minton, Balch and Co., 1928.

Jefferson Davis: His Rise and Fall. New York: Minton, Balch and Co., 1929.

Poems: 1928-1931. New York and London: Charles Scribner's Sons, 1932.

Reactionary Essays on Poetry and Ideas. New York: Charles Scribner's Sons, 1936.

The Mediterranean and Other Poems. New York: Alcestis Press, 1936.

Selected Poems. New York and London: Charles Scribner's Sons, 1937.

The Fathers. New York: G. P. Putnam's Sons, 1938.

Reason in Madness, Critical Essays. New York: G. P. Putnam's Sons, 1941.

The Vigil of Venus. Cummington, Massachusetts: Cummington Press, 1943.

The Winter Sea. Cummington, Massachusetts: Cummington Press, 1944.

Poems: 1922-1947. New York: Charles Scribner's Sons, 1948.

On the Limits of Poetry, Selected Essays 1928-1948. New York: The Swallow Press and William Morrow and Co., 1948.

The Hovering Fly and Other Essays. Cummington, Massachusetts: Cummington Press, 1949.

Two Conceits for the Eye to Sing, if Possible. Cummington, Massachusetts: Cummington Press, 1950.

The Forlorn Demon: Didactic and Critical Essays. Chicago: Henry Regnery Co., 1953.

The Man of Letters in the Modern World, Selected Essays: 1928-1955. New York: Meridian Books, 1955.

Collected Essays. Denver: Alan Swallow, 1959.

Poems. New York: Charles Scribner's Sons, 1960.

B. *Books Edited*

I'll Take My Stand; The South and the Agrarian Tradition, by Twelve Southerners. New York and London: Harper and Bros., 1930.

Who Owns America? A Declaration of Independence, ed. HERBERT AGAR and ALLEN TATE. Boston and New York: Houghton Mifflin Co., 1936.

The Language of Poetry. Princeton: Princeton University Press and London: Oxford University Press, 1942.

Princeton Verse Between Two Wars. Princeton: Princeton University Press, 1942.

American Harvest: Twenty Years of Creative Writing in the United States, ed. ALLEN TATE and JOHN PEALE BISHOP. New York: L. B. Fischer, 1942.

Sixty American Poets, 1896-1944, a Checklist. Washington, 1945.

A Southern Vanguard. New York: Prentice-Hall, 1947.

The Collected Poems of John Peale Bishop, 1892-1944. New York: Charles Scribner's Sons, 1948.

The House of Fiction: An Anthology of the Short Story, ed. CAROLINE GORDON and ALLEN TATE. New York: Charles Scribner's Sons, 1950.

Modern Verse in English, 1900-1950, ed. DAVID CECIL and ALLEN TATE. New York: The Macmillan Company, 1958.

C. *Selected Periodical Publications*

"A Ballade of the Lugubrious Wench," *Jade,* III (November 12, 1921), 17.

"To Intellectual Detachment," *The Fugitive,* I (April, 1922), 9.

"Sinbad," *The Fugitive,* I (April, 1922), 16.

"Farewell to Anactoria," *The Fugitive,* I (June, 1922), 39.

"In Secret Valley," *The Fugitive,* I (June, 1922), 57.

"To Oenia in Wintertime," *The Fugitive,* I (October, 1922), 71.

"Horatian Epode to the Duchess of Malfi," *The Fugitive,* I (October, 1922), 76.

"The Happy Poet Remembers Death," *The Fugitive,* II (April-May, 1923), 54.

"The Screen," *The Fugitive,* II (June-July, 1923), 70-71.

"Procession," *The Fugitive,* II (June-July, 1923), 83.

"One Escape from the Dilemma," *The Fugitive,* III (April, 1924), 34-36.

"Correspondences (From the French of Charles Baudelaire)," *The Fugitive,* III (December, 1924), 133.

"Homily," *The Fugitive,* IV (March, 1925), 11.

"Last Days of a Charming Lady," *Nation,* CXXI (October 28, 1925), 485-86.

"A Poetry of Ideas," *New Republic,* XLVII (June 30, 1926), 172-73.

"Poetry and the Absolute," *Sewanee Review,* XXXV (January, 1927), 41-52.

"The Revolt Against Literature," *New Republic,* XLIX (February 9, 1927), 329-30.

"A Tendency Yearbook," *Bookman,* LXVIII (November, 1928), 353-55.

"American Poetry Since 1920," *Bookman,* LXVIII (January, 1929), 503-8.

"The Fallacy of Humanism," *Hound and Horn,* III (January, 1930), 234-57.

"Confusion and Poetry," *Sewanee Review,* XXXVIII (April, 1930), 133-49.

"Post-Symbolism," *Hound and Horn,* IV (June, 1931), 619-24.

"Regionalism and Sectionalism," *New Republic,* LXIX (December 23, 1931), 158-61.

"The Whole Image of Man," *Hound and Horn,* VI (January, 1933), 345-49.

"The Immortal Woman," *Hound and Horn,* VI (July, 1933), 592-609.

"Poetry and Politics," *New Republic,* LXXV (August 2, 1933), 308-11.

"The Migration," *Yale Review,* XXIV (September, 1934), 83-111.

"The Fugitive—1922-1925," *Princeton University Library Chronicle,* III (April, 1942), 75-84.

"The Post of Observation in Fiction," *Maryland Quarterly*, II (1944), 61-64.

"Homage to St.-John Perse," *Poetry*, LXXV (January, 1950), 213-16.

"Three Commentaries: Poe, James, and Joyce," *Sewanee Review*, LVIII (Winter, 1950), 1-15.

"Orthodoxy and the Standard of Literature," *New Republic*, CXXVIII (January 5, 1953), 24-25.

"Clarity, Elegance and Power," *New Republic*, CXXVIII (March 2, 1953), 17-18.

"Self-Made Angel," *New Republic*, CXXIX (August 31, 1953), 17-18.

"Christ and the Unicorn," *Sewanee Review*, LXIII (April, 1955), 175-81.

"Reflections on American Poetry, 1900-1950," *Sewanee Review*, LXIV (January, 1956), 59-70.

"The Novel in the American South," *New Statesman*, LVII (June 13, 1959), 831-32.

"A Great Stylist: the Prophet as Critic," *Sewanee Review*, LXIX (Spring, 1961), 314-17.

"The Gaze Past, The Glance Present," *Sewanee Review*, LXX (Autumn, 1962), 671-73.

"For John Ransom at Seventy-Five," *Shenandoah*, XIV (Summer, 1963), 5-8.

"In Memoriam Theodore Roethke 1908-1963," *Encounter*, XX, no. 121, p. 68.

"William Faulkner 1897-1962," *Sewanee Review*, LXXI, (1963), 160-64.

"Shadow: A Parable, and a Polemic," *National Poetry Festival, Held in the Library of Congress, October 22-24, 1962—Proceedings*. Washington: Library of Congress, 1964, pp. 271-74.

SECONDARY SOURCES

AMYX, CLIFFORD. "The Aesthetics of Allen Tate," *Western Review*, XIII (Spring, 1949), 135-44. Finds Tate's conception of tension in poetry much better than his earlier "intensification beyond the moral situation."

BEATTY, RICHMOND C. "Allen Tate as a Man of Letters," *South Atlantic Quarterly*, XLVII, (April, 1948), 226-41. Approaches Tate's poetry from the point of view of his own critical observations.

BERLAND, ALWYN. "Violence in the Poetry of Allen Tate," *Accent*, XI (Summer, 1951), 161-71. Finds Tate "obsessed by vision of chaos."

BLACKMUR, R. P. "*San Giovanni in Venere*: Allen Tate as Man of Letters," *Sewanee Review*, LXVII (Autumn, 1959), 614-31. Tate's mind operates "as if all necessary theory had been received into his bones and blood before birth."

BRADBURY, JOHN M. *The Fugitives: A Critical Account*. Chapel Hill: The University of North Carolina Press, 1958. Useful survey; marred by failure to come to grips with many of the basic essentials of Tate's work.

————. *Renaissance in the South*. Chapel Hill: The University of North Carolina Press, 1963. Survey.

BROOKS, CLEANTH. "Allen Tate," *Poetry*, LXVI (September, 1945), 324-29. Excellent review-essay of *The Winter Sea*.

COWAN, LOUISE. *The Fugitive Group: A Literary History*. Baton Rouge: Louisiana State University Press, 1959. Admirably detailed account of the Fugitive period.

COWLEY, MALCOLM. "Two Winters with Hart Crane," *Sewanee Review*, LXVII (Autumn, 1959), 547-56. Personal reminiscence.

DAVIS, ROBERT GORHAM. "The New Criticism and the Democratic Tradition," *American Scholar*, XIX (Winter, 1950), 9-19. Finds the program of the "New Critics" preposterous for a democratic society.

FEDER, LILLIAN. "Allen Tate's Use of Classical Literature," *The Centennial Review*, IV (Winter, 1960), 89-114. Finds Tate's Classicism "in his way of thought and of feeling in poetry."

FLEMING, RUDD. "Dramatic Involution: Tate, Husserl, and Joyce," *Sewanee Review*, LX (Summer, 1952), 445-64. Discusses Tate's change of "vantage point" in the light of Husserl's "phenomenological epoché."

FOSTER, RICHARD. "Narcissus as Pilgrim: Allen Tate," *Accent*, XVII (Summer, 1957), 158-71. States that purpose is to exhibit Tate's romanticism.

————. *The New Romantics: A Reappraisal of the New Criticism*. Bloomington: Indiana University Press, 1962. Provocative.

GLICKSBERG, CHARLES I. "Allen Tate and Mother Earth," *Sewanee Review*, XLVIII (July, 1937), 315-21. Finds Tate guilty of "treason to intellectuals."

GREENHUT, MORRIS. "Sources of Obscurity in Modern Poetry: The Examples of Eliot, Stevens, and Tate," *Centennial Review of Arts and Sciences*, VII (1963), 171-90. Finds title, musical structure, and imagery of Tate's "Ode" confusing. Slight.

HEMPHILL, GEORGE. *Allen Tate* (UMPAW, 39). Minneapolis: University of Minnesota Press, 1964. Proposes to correct the view of Tate as a professional Southerner. Good brief introduction; sometimes rather flippant.

JOHNSON, CAROL. "The Heroism of the Rational: the Poetry of Allen Tate," *Renascence*, XVII (1963), 89-96. Finds that in Tate's "attention to the task at hand lies the heroism of the rational."

KERMODE, FRANK. "The Dissociation of Sensibility," *Kenyon Review*, XIX (Spring, 1957), 169-94. Discusses the history of the concept. Finds modern authors abandoning the idea.

————. "Old Orders Changing," *Encounter*, XV (August, 1960), 72-76. Review-essay of *The Fathers* and of *The Leopard* by Giuseppe di Lampedusa. Praises Tate's ability to have his images accrete significance throughout the novel.

————. "Contemplation and Method," *Sewanee Review*, LXXII (1963), Review-essay of *The Last Alternatives*. Finds it method-ridden.

KNICKERBOCKER, W. C. "Friction of Powder Puffs; Tatian Esoterics," *Sewanee Review*, XLVIII (July, 1940), 315-21. Notes on *The Golden Mean*.

KOCH, VIVIENNE. "The Poetry of Allen Tate," *Kenyon Review*, XI (Summer,

1949), 355-78. Finds Tate "practitioner of this awesome and marvelous feat of poetic balance between the classic and romantic, the metaphysical and the symbolist."

MEINERS, R. K. *The Last Alternatives: A Study of the Works of Allen Tate.* Denver: Alan Swallow, 1962. Good insights into Tate's use of symbols, unfortunately couched in an exasperatingly personal style.

MIZENER, ARTHUR. "*The Fathers* and Realistic Fiction," *Accent,* VII (Winter, 1947), 101-9. Stresses the function of the double consciousness of Lacy Buchan.

NEMEROV, HOWARD. "The Current of the Frozen Stream: An Essay on the Poetry of Allen Tate," *Furioso,* III (February, 1948), 50-61. Finds that the major themes of Tate's poems is "man's attachment to the past."

RANSOM, JOHN CROWE. "*In Amicitia,*" *Sewanee Review,* LXVII, (Autumn, 1959), 528-39. Comments on Tate's intellectual development.

RUBIN, LOUIS D. "The Serpent in the Mulberry Bush," *Southern Renascence: the Literature of the Modern South.* Baltimore: The Johns Hopkins Press, 1953, pp. 352-67. Finds Tate's poems the mirror of his own problems.

————. "Allen Tate: The Arrogant Circumstance," *South: Modern Southern Literature in its Cultural Setting,* ed. LOUIS D. RUBIN and ROBERT D. JACOBS. Garden City, N. Y. Doubleday and Company, 1961, pp. 221-47. Tate described as one of the "seminal poets of the twentieth century."

————. *The Faraway Country.* Seattle: The University of Washington Press, 1963. Tate discussed under "The Poetry of Agrarianism."

SCHWARTZ, DELMORE. "The Poetry of Allen Tate," *Southern Review,* V (Winter, 1940), 419-38. Finds Tate too oblique, narrow, and over-concentrated.

"Southern Style," *Times Literary Supplement,* August 5, 1960, p. 496. Review-essay of the English republication of *The Fathers.* Affords it high praise both for its perceptiveness of social issues and for its style.

SMITH, JANET ADAM. "The End of the Old Dominion," *New Statesman,* LIX (May 14, 1960), 763-65. Review of *The Fathers,* praising it as one of the more significant novels of our time.

SPEARS, MONROE K. "The Criticism of Allen Tate," *Sewanee Review,* LXVII (Spring, 1949), 317-34. Analysis of Tate as a polemical critic opposed to positivism.

STEWART, JOHN L. *The Burden of Time: The Fugitives and Agrarians.* Princeton: Princeton University Press, 1965. Disproportionate attention to Tate's early poems.

THORP, WILLARD. "Allen Tate: A Checklist," *Princeton University Library Chronicle,* III (April, 1942), 85-98. Indispensable bibliographical study.

VIVAS, ELISEO. "Allen Tate as Man of Letters," *Sewanee Review,* LXII (Winter, 1954), 131-43. Discusses Tate's criticism as emanating from the pose of "man of letters."

Index

Index